Rock-climbing communities of practice: physical and digital encounters

An imprint of Boom Publications Ltd
272 Bath Street
Glasgow SCOTLAND
G2 4JR

Boom Graduates and the logo are trademarks of Boom Publications Ltd.

Boom Publications Ltd is a more-than-profit company, dedicating over half our profits to university scholarships for underprivileged students worldwide.
In order to offset our carbon footprint, we also pledge to plant a tree for each graduation book commissioned.

Rock-climbing and communities of practice: physical and digital encounters
was first published in Great Britain in 2022.

Boom Publications Ltd do not have any control over, or responsibility for any third-party websites referred to or in this book. All internet addresses given in this book were correct at the time of going to press. The author and publisher regret any inconvenience if addresses have changed or sites have ceased to exist, but can accept no responsibility for any such changes.

Typeset by Helen at Boom Graduates.
Printed and bound in the UK.

ISBN: 9798838405289

To find out more about our authors and books visit www.boompublications.com and sign up for our newsletters and special offers.

Rock-climbing communities of practice: physical and digital encounters

Rock-climbing communities of practice: physical and digital encounters

Table of contents

Author's acknowledgements

I would like to use this space to say thank you and share my experience in writing this book. Being in and out of a hospital, whether serious or not, gives you the space and time to reflect on the people that really matter to you. This research project has helped me motivate myself through some of the strangest times I have experienced thus far in my life, taking place during the Covid-19 era, and when I was hospitalised on three separate occasions including a scheduled operation, a serious burn, and a car crash. I have shouted, smiled, cried, laughed, given up, started again, doubted myself, and doubted my future. However, the most important lesson I can take from the last eight months is building confidence underneath my own skin. When everything appears to 'go wrong', at the end of it, you open your eyes, you're still alive, and you made it through, graceful or not. I'm grateful for everyone at Leeds Beckett University who helped me build my confidence and remained psyched for me throughout. No matter how many years it took me to string a sentence together, or to speak in front of other people without feeling nervous, all the lecturers constantly saw my potential, and it has changed my life. A warm thank you to my family: Helen (mum), Leon, and Paul, my lecturers: Zoe and Jayne, and my disability support worker, Matt.

Author biography

Matt Green holds a First Class BA (Hons) in Media Communication Cultures, and a Masters with Distinction in Media and Culture from Leeds Beckett University. His research focuses on the social science of sports, through communities of practice, and gender studies. Matt is an avid rock-climber and boulderer, and teaches climbing at a prominent bouldering wall in the north of England where he is based.

Abstract

Unexplored previously by scholars, neoliberal values are manifested into social norms through alternative cultures which intend to 'liberate' from the operations of everyday life. The study of the social behaviour of rock-climbers, and how they are operated by media artefacts such as documentaries and vlogs remain undeveloped. Taking this into account, it is important to investigate how new media contributes towards cultural governance and social behaviour. From this perspective, the concept of neoliberalism is more than just a tool of social-economic control. To develop a critical account of Foucault (2008) and Beck's (1991) work, this study suggests that neoliberalism controls social behaviour through the universal fear of risk in modern society. Human activity is therefore organised through neoliberalism's individualised entrepreneurship. Through this, human groups naturally resist society's structural organisation by cultivating their own unique way of living. Csikzentmihalyi's (1990) concept of flow has an explanatory power that demonstrates how climbers are able to immerse themselves in moments of non-thinking. Through this, climbers push the boundaries of their physical capability by confronting fear through in-depth focus. Finally, the study argues that 'neoliberal competition' is deeply embedded into modern human behaviour, even within alternative sporting cultures such as rock-climbing.

Introduction

This study produces a critical understanding of neoliberalism (Foucault, 2008), risk societies (Beck, 2014), and flow (Csikszentmihalyi, 1990) through rock-climbing vlogs. The book suggests that the dynamics of modern life prevent individuals from experiencing flow state (Csikszentmihalyi, 1990). In doing so, climbers immerse themselves in the flow state to resist the risk-averse lifestyle associated with neoliberal values. The study will emphasise the effects of social behaviour, and how people use social memberships to attach themselves to groups of equivalence. Despite rock-climbing's resistance against governance, it is important to note that climbing behaviours are still associated with neoliberalism through the notion of deeply embedded competition. Through this, the book suggests that social interactions impact the wider context of rock-climbing cultures through the competitive norms produced by neoliberalism.

Literature Review

The literature review suggests that outdoor rock-climbing enables people to resist universal social norms within modern society through the experience of risk. The chapter uses three key writers to investigate flow theory's relevance to risk-taking in contemporary rock-climbing media. Foucault's (2008) perspective of neoliberalism helps to explain how individualised entrepreneurship manipulates people's instinctive human nature. Beck's (2014) risk-free society will be applied to analyse people's attraction towards risky leisure pursuits. Finally, Csikszentmihalyi's (1990) theory of flow will discuss how human consciousness is affected by cultural and behavioural norms produced by neoliberalism. Throughout the chapter, social norms will be used to investigate the construction of 'acceptable' behaviours in modern society (McDonald et al., 2017).

The chapter will investigate flow and its relevance to risk-taking in contemporary rock-climbing media through climbing vlogs. Through this, it becomes clear that climbing media is used to escape from cultural and behavioural norms produced by neoliberal governance. The chapter investigates competition, and how this emerges from social norms that are collectively organised by neoliberal governance (Read, 2009; Beattie, 2019). To support this, Foucault's (2008) homo-economicus will be challenged by Beck's (2014) reading on the structural dynamics of the modern world. This suggests that human activity is organised and controlled through individualised entrepreneurship (Beck, 2014). This is significant because the notion of 'risk' has become central within governed societies through economics, individualised security, and the pursuit of self-interest (Beck, 1991). The chapter will then explain the significance of rock-climbing vlogs, and how they produce access for wider audiences. To justify this, the chapter argues that the structure of modern life prevents individuals from immersing themselves in flow state, which shares an intrinsic relationship with rock-climbing (Csikszentmihalyi, 1990). Finally, this chapter argues that some individuals engage with rock-climbing to resist risk-averse lifestyles, despite its relationship with individualised competition.

Methodology

The Methodology section discusses the methods used to investigate climbing vlogs and their purpose as a cultural learning tool. The study uses the video elicitation method alongside 'climb-along' interviews. Further, the chapter explains how these methods enable the study to explore recurring themes for further analysis in the findings and discussion chapter. The qualitative method is justified by investigating how contemporary social behaviour in rock-climbing vlogs impacts upon everyday human experiences. Through the interviews, the study investigates how climbers recreate their own unique climbing lifestyles through climbing vlogs. 'Climb-along' interviews are used in this research method to illustrate the sensory experience of fear. This is carried out by discussing the participant's personal experiences in climbing locations. Climb-along interviews allow the study to investigate the 'real-life' and mediated understanding of social behaviour in rock-climbing communities. In doing so, the interview process is separated into two halves. The first half delves into the participants' overall thoughts about rock-climbing vlogs, and the lifestyle of rock-climbing cultures. The participants then watch three climbing vlogs created by Magnus Midtbo, Adam Ondra, and Anna Hazlenutt. The second half of the interview monitors how the participant's perception of risk changes after watching the climbing vlogs. This enables the study to develop various types, trends, and themes for chapter three, the findings, and discussion chapter. Further, the study also ensures that age and gender diversity is incorporated into the sampling strategy of the methodology.

Findings and Discussion

The findings and discussion chapter discuss the qualitative data found in the 'climb-along' interviews. The chapter organises the qualitative findings into three themes to ensure that the study's key points are clearly organised. Through this, the study is able to clearly assess the relationship between rock-climbing and modern media texts. To ensure consistency, material found in chapter two, the literature review, will be included in the findings and discussion chapter. This ensures that neoliberalism (Foucault, 2008), risk (Beck, 1991), and flow (Csikszentmihalyi, 1990) are embedded into the study's main discussion. Through social connections, the theme of Risk suggests that climbers develop their repertoire of climbing experiences through their commitment to various rock-climbing communities. The theme of risk argues that climbers are motivated to develop their climbing experience through the climbers and friends in their chosen communities. It is important to consider that involvement in a rock-climbing community requires years of commitment. Therefore, climbing vlogs create effortless access to online rock-climbing communities. Through this, the theme suggests that risk is reconstructed into a cultural and collective experience through climbing vlogs. The theme of Media Intimacy investigates the development of online communication, and how it encourages an inclusive rock-climbing environment. Whilst climbing vlogs invoke an encouraging environment, it will become clear that elitism is a natural part of real-life rock-climbing through competitive behaviour types. In doing so, 'intimacy' in a digital and real-life context creates spaces for unique relationships. This provides evidence that rock-climbing social behaviours arise from competitive norms within real-life rock-climbing venues. The theme of Social Regulation suggests that social norms and behaviours also emerge from rock-climbing's immerse practice. Through this, it will become clear that machoism and 'showing no fear' have become intrinsically connected to rock-climbing's cultural performance. The theme will suggest that individuals attach themselves to groups of equivalence in rock-climbing social spheres. Through this, some climbers are still bound to the neoliberal 'frame of mind' through competition and elitism. This study produces a critical understanding of neoliberalism (Foucault, 2008), risk societies (Beck, 2014), and flow (Csikszentmihalyi, 1990) through rock-climbing vlogs. This will suggest that the dynamics of modern life prevent individuals from experiencing flow state (Csikszentmihalyi, 1990). In doing so, climbers immerse themselves in the flow state to resist the risk-averse lifestyle associated with neoliberal values. The study emphasises the effects of social behaviour, and how people use social memberships to attach themselves to groups of equivalence. Despite rock-climbing's resistance against governance, it is important to note that climbing behaviours are still associated with neoliberalism through the notion of deeply embedded competition. Through this, the study will suggest that social interactions impact the wider context of rock-climbing cultures through the competitive norms produced by neoliberalism.

Csikzentmihalyi's (1990) flow is intrinsically connected to neoliberalism through individualised thinking and contemporary social behaviour. In doing so, this book is written in line with

Foucault (2008) to suggest that governance has the power to operate the everyday lives of modern citizens. Some may argue that Goffman's (1963) social behaviour demonstrates a clearer understanding of alternative climbing cultures. However, the notion of governance will suggest that neoliberalism is still deeply embedded into the modern state of 'being', despite rock-climbing's cultural resistance against the operations of everyday life.

What is flow and its relevance to risk-taking in contemporary rock-climbing media?

This literature review argues that rock-climbing enables people to challenge normative ways of living by experiencing risk in various outdoor climbing scenarios. The ideology of neoliberalism is used to suggest that individuals are restricted from experiencing risk because of secure lifestyles, which are embedded into modern ways of living. By drawing on Foucault (2008), it is clear that people have become more accountable for their own security based on neoliberal's subjectivation procedure. Therefore, the chances of engaging with outdoor rock climbing and its accompanying of risk have arguably become rare in the context of wider society. Foucault's (2008) concept of the homo economicus individual will be included to explain how risk-taking can be viewed as a voluntary choice in modern society, which is said to emerge from the desire of freedom. Further, Beck's (1991) risk free society will contribute to this by suggesting that the more safe and risk-free ordinary life becomes, the more that risky leisure pursuits become attractive. The notion of security involves stationary and immobilised lives, this will be challenged through the emergence of a climber's relationship with 'van life' and travelling. This will challenge Pinson and Journel's (2016) immobile neoliberal city, because the impact of remote working now allows individuals to travel and climb whilst maintaining their individualised security. The literature review will be primarily focused on traditional constraints and social norms, these concepts will be used to elicit the cultural restriction of mobilised climbing lifestyles. Habitual identities (Bourdieu, 1984) have also been included in the literature review to explain how global transformations produce various privileges and divide social classes into separate communities. Csikszentmihalyi's (1990) theory of flow is included to characterise the mental and physical demands of rock-climbing, and their relationship with emotional release. Flow will allow the chapter to discuss how human consciousness is affected by neoliberalism. This will suggest that neoliberalism prevents individuals from experiencing flow state, restricting individuals from experiencing the immediate and intrinsic awards of outdoor rock climbing. This is significant because risk societies do not hold some individuals back from placing their bodies at immediate risk on outdoor climbing routes. A climbing route is a line of holds which can be climbed by a human body up a natural rock face - these can soloed, placed with protection on higher routes, or bouldered on shorter routes. The literature review will finally investigate how access to outdoor climbing is produced, arguing that online climbing vlogs allow individuals to develop new and existing abilities through online learning. In doing so, the literature review provides evidence that climbing vlog audiences are significant because they able to develop experience and knowledge through digital media and assign them into real-life climbing scenarios.

Neoliberalism organises every element of a person's time by exchanging working hours for safety and secure living through individualised entrepreneurship (Chesire and Lawrence, 2006). The ideology of neoliberalism suggests that modern citizens have been restricted to organised lifestyles that prioritise personal financial gains over the experience of subjective human nature. According to Foucault (2008, p.226), 'in neo-liberalism, the homo economicus is an entrepreneur of himself... being for himself his own capital, being for himself his own producer'. Homo economicus defines the behaviour associated with individualised self-interest, which influences modern citizens to exchange working hours for personalised security. An organised lifestyle is the result of governmental neoliberal regulations, and in this instance, the only way to organise human activity within a nation is through individualised entrepreneurship (Beck, 2014). Through neoliberalism, people are being produced as subjects of 'human capital', replacing the notion of exchange with competition (Read, 2009; and Beattie, 2019). It is important to note that the collective organisation of modern economics ensures that the structure of society does not financially collapse. In doing so, the impact of economic thinking influences people to invest in self-interest and hyper-organised lifestyles (Laval, 2017) rather than immersing themselves in the wider context of life experience. By reducing government spending, the citizens of a nation witness the expansion of privatisation, austerity, and globalised markets. However, the notion of a universal market (whereby governmental spending is reduced) influences people to 'adapt and compete' for resources.

Neoliberalism does not consider the implications of a lifestyle exempt from economic responsibility, and how it would impact on the day-to-day workings of individual lives.

The pursuit of self-interest influences individuals to work within their corporate spheres more efficiently, knowing that personal benefit is found by ambitiously climbing the corporate ladder. From neoliberalism's perspective, individuals compete for wealth and resources by contributing towards a capital market by working within privatised firms and developing themselves in professional spheres. The term 'resource' refers to an individual's access to a functional living space, reasonable living expenditure, and overall job security. This is significant because Hanley (2011, p.3) suggests that these resources are becoming more difficult to access since the 2008 global financial crisis. Through this, the notion of personal responsibility has become a shared value in public and private domains. This suggests that 'personal lives are being monitored in the name of security' (Braedley and Luxton, 2010, p.198) in so-called modern welfare states. In this instance, the ideology of neoliberalism implies that communities of people and non-profit sectors (mutual businesses, social enterprises, and charities) work alongside each other because they are held accountable for their own security and the security of their nation.

Despite the importance of national security and its relationship with individualised contribution, the lifestyle of rock-climbing may emerge from the desire for freedom because of Beck's (1991) risk free society. Beck (1991) argues that the notion of risk is becoming increasingly central to our global society. Technological advances and security measures ensure that the potential threats that people face in day-to-day life are diminished. However, the more safe and risk-free ordinary life becomes, the more that risky leisure pursuits become attractive. Developing and maintaining security is embedded in the modernised lifestyle, which affects the lives of many individuals and modern society as a collective experience. 'Reducing risk to life and distributing the economic costs of risks' in the modernised and industrial world is a primary concern of modern governments (Simon, 2001, p.177). Beck (2014, p.12) contributes towards the 'risk-free' society by suggesting that 'global risk' encourages the 'omnipresence of media', which normalises death and suffering as a collective experience. The collective experience of media stories produces anxiety amongst various nations, influencing people to minimise the chance of risk in their day-to-day lives. In doing so, individuals are influenced to avoid 'death and suffering' by competing for essential resources in a risk-free society, which exchanges personal freedom and working hours for 'safe living'. Risk in a neoliberal context is also viewed as the struggle for resources, for example, food, housing, and dental and medical appointments, rather than a direct and immediate threat to someone's life. In this instance, outdoor rock-climbing is significant because direct and immediate threats to an individual's life can occur during any climb or expedition (Griffin, 2012; Herrera, 2002). Activities such as rock-climbing and mountaineering, which involve the risk of injury and death, have become an expression of escape for individuals who desire exposure to the natural human experience. Some individuals use high-pressure job roles to significantly decrease the chance of homelessness and danger. However, for renowned Yosemite climbers such as Ron Kauk, Doug Robinson, John Long, and Lynn Hill, abject poverty did not stop them from dedicating their younger lives to rock climbing. In Valley Uprising (2014), Doug Robinson states that 'in mainstream America, safety and comfort were the primary values, there wasn't any outlet for the spirit of adventure'. For the climbers of Yosemite Valley in the 1970s, living in rock formations and physical danger associated with free soloing and traditional climbing were embodied into everyday life. This suggests that cultures centred around risk avoidance do not allow various individuals to express themselves in their natural human spirit. However, the media representations of behaviour associated with risk-averse lifestyles are often highly correlated with machoism and Class-A drug use in documentaries of historic rock-climbing (Valley Uprising, 2014). Despite the adverse media perspective of a climbing life, different scholars have recorded the emergence of new behaviours and desires which arise from the practice of rock-climbing.

The practice of rock-climbing is also intrinsically connected with the social life of rock-climbing. This is significant because climbing as an individualised practice can be shared with other people and understood through Wenger's (2011) concept of communities of practice. In doing so, this allows climbers to produce shared objectives of contemporary climbing routes and use media to source new challenges and share knowledge about different styles of climbing and body movement. According to Wenger (2011, p.1) 'communities of practice are formed by people who engage in a process of collective learning in a shared domain of human endeavours'. Through Wenger's (2011; Luckin and Wetherby, 2014) communities of practice, climbers can use media to source new routes, climbing techniques, and objectives to escape from the responsibilities of everyday life. This is evidenced by Kenyon (1968, p.101), who suggests that outdoor climbing allows individuals to 'release frustration and pent-up emotions created by the pressure of modern living'. In doing so, the risk associated with outdoor rock-climbing lifestyles can be viewed as a form of diverse expression against risk avoidance in competition-driven neoliberalist lifestyles.

The practice of outdoor climbing challenges Pinson and Journel's (2016) 'neoliberal city' because of its relationship with 'van life' and travelling. 'Van life' consists of converting transit vans into spaces for living to enable consistent travel across geographical locations for all-season climbing. This challenges the stationary nature of urban living, which is based on Pinson and Journel's (2016, p.138) suggestion that western cities are the centre of social structures, economic functions, and governance. The term globalisation 'changes human relationships and refers to a transformation in the dimensions of time and space between people and places, and amongst organisations, institutions, nations, and cultures' (Elliot and Urry, 2010, p.87). Through globalisation, climbers can commute between different interdependent economies and populations. Globalisation has a strong relationship with the travelling, climbing, and vlog lifestyle because to carry out this lifestyle, an individual must be unhooked and dis-embedded from traditional constraints (Elliot and Urry, 2010; Llopis-Goig, 2016). Subcultures can be defined as a cultural group characterised by various and alternative beliefs and interests outside of universal norms (Hebdige, 1979). Traditional constraints define the traits and behaviours adopted by repetitious social norms, all of which are culturally adopted by different human groups. For example, the limited stimulus of urban leisure is governed by theatres, bars, alcohol, and retail to soothe the mental and physical aspects of the body. Although some sports activities are found in urban space, the social life associated with urban leisure has a strong relationship with liberty and pleasure, rather than self-improvement. This is evidenced by Winlow and Hall (2006, p.80) who suggests that leisure 'appears to have been a component part in a complex process that has gradually produced an increasingly divided and polarised contemporary social life'. Both recreational and urban leisure are a natural response to traditional constraints, which confine individuals into specific living styles. In doing so, leisure in its wider scope can be used as a source to escape traditional constraints for short periods of time.

Traditional constraints produce social norms which restrict individuals from exposing themselves to diverse lifestyles, such as outdoor rock-climbing. The restriction of lifestyles emerges from the aesthetic preference of different social classes, which influences how people construct their social reality (Argyle, 1994; McDonald et al., 2017). In doing so, traditional constraints define how established western cultures sustain the resistance of cultural change (Toh and Leonardelli, 2012). Traditional constraints are organised by social norms: socially agreed standards which guide people's behaviour on all levels of social organisation (Gelfand, 2018; Hechter and Opp,

2001). This is significant because risk avoidance is embedded into contemporary western social norms (Bunn, 2017). In this instance, wellbeing instructs individuals to avoid risk-taking behaviours and activities (Goudie, et al., 2014). Yet Goudie et al. (2014) have not considered the diverse motives behind risk-taking behaviour, which are based on the supposition that putting the body in physical risk implies low wellbeing. Conversely, Crust (2020, p.2) suggests that mountaineers and outdoor traditional climbers 'possess a need for stimulation (e.g., thrill and excitement)'. This is significant because climbers who execute rare and outstanding achievements use risk, stimulation, and socially mobile living styles to accomplish their goals. This is evidenced by high profile free solo climber Alex Honnold's regular exposure to physical danger and mobile accommodation, which allowed him to execute his free solo ascent of Free Rider on El Capitan (Free Solo, 2017). High profile YouTube climber Pete Whittaker has rope soloed El Capitan's Free Rider and published his achievements by sharing his knowledge through online instructional vlogs (Wide Boyz, 2021). Rare and adventurous lifestyles presented in contemporary climbing vlogs are enabled by the shift from traditional and stationary constraints to socially mobile and risk induced living. This could also be caused by new media, and its shift towards user generated content. In this instance, rock-climbing content can be shared onto social media platforms, which in return can produce cultural change (Jenkins et al., 2016).

Some climbing names have enhanced their popularity by presenting vlog audiences with diverse climbing locations across the globe, enabled by the emergence of flexible and cheap international travel (Elliot and Urry, 2010). Alternative climbing lifestyles respond to contemporary global transformations by challenging 'habitual identities'. Habitual identities shape current practices and structures which condition people's perception of place (Bourdieu, 1984). Through this, communities become stationary and networked, influenced by their cultural history. According to Frykman and Lofgren (1996, p.10), 'habits organise life for individuals, linking them to groups so that cultural community is often established by people together tackling the world around them with familiar manoeuvres'. Some scholars suggest that modern human behaviour has progressed from habitual identities into a culture of mobilised living. Western and capitalist societies use tourism to globalise the world for mobile consumers (Bianchi, 2006). However, this statement does not consider the implications of social class and its relationship with globalised mobility. This is because those from lower economic backgrounds are limited to habitual identities. This is evidenced by Castells (1996), who suggests that mobility can be seen as a marker of privilege and power. In doing so, various climbing vlogs demonstrate that the mobile terrain of the climbing lifestyle is centred around exploring new environments and travelling between different networked communities of climbers. It is important to note that rock-climbing and its relationship with mobility cannot be applied to lower working classes which are restricted to habitual identities (Tyler, 2020). However, climbing vlogs demonstrate that new and inventive leisure lifestyles are capable of deconstructing traditional habitual identities for individuals who have access to globalised mobility. This assumes that various individuals in privileged class systems may live within the comfort of their own social spheres from birth, rather than using mobility as an opportunity to explore. Although habitual identities still exist within the modern world, globalisation could influence people's ambitions within various spheres of leisure. In doing so, the social life which surrounds climbing may also influence people's lifestyles because of its relationship with non-thinking. Climbing and its relationship with non-thinking is known to reduce stress and influence wider lifestyle choices, such as increased time in nature and working towards climbing objectives through intensive training routines.

Climbing has a strong relationship with Csikszentmihalyi's (1990) Flow, a theory that explains how individuals experience states of concentration whilst carrying out challenging activities. Csikszentmihalyi (1997; Garrido-Palomino and Espana-Romero, 2019) suggests that an individual can experience flow when various skills are used to complete a difficult task. Csikszentihalyi (2014) is interested in the recurring experience of flow in leisure activities. He draws on the experience of a university professor to outline 'flow state' during rock-climbing: "When I start to climb, it's as if my memory input has been cut off. All I can remember is the last thirty seconds, and all I can think ahead is the next five minutes... With tremendous concentration, the normal world is forgotten" (Csikszentilhalyi, 2014, p.7). When the world is 'shut off and forgotten' during a leisure activity, the individual experiences a condition called 'optimal experience'. Optimal experiences are made possible by an unusually intense concentration on a limited stimulus field (Csikszentihalyi, 2014, p.7). A stimulus field is a leisure activity which limits the physical body to different types of movement whilst focusing on the achievement of a specific objective. However, the concept of optimal experience has been criticised because productivity can be viewed as a process of distraction, 'a coping mechanism for a brutal situation, akin to workaholics' (Hujich, 2012). Although the optimal experience is symbolic of avoidance, Hujich (2012) does not consider leisure as a non-work activity in the discipline of self-improvement. The term leisure can encompass recreational sport as well as mundane non-work activities such as drinking, smoking, and making love (Featherstone, 1985, p.113). Whilst leisure activities have been viewed as a process of distraction, optimal flow and its relationship with climbing is significant because it exposes individuals to 'intense emotions' (Luttenberger et al., 2015, p.2). Csikszentmihalyi (2014) uses the release of intense emotion in leisure to foreground the importance of human consciousness and how it is used autonomously in day-to-day life. From this perspective, an individual is 'free to decide what feeling they shall place in the focus of their consciousness' (Collingwood, 1938, p.207). The limited stimulus field experienced during activities such as climbing allows individuals to engage with non-thinking, a synergy of focus, physical danger, and body movement.

According to neoliberalism, modern life prevents individuals from experiencing different types of flow states, as the management of consciousness could be affected by the lifestyle of neoliberalism. Although some aspects of neoliberal lifestyles are moving towards cyberspace to create flexibility, workers are still consumed by 30.3% longer working hours (Cameron, 2020) despite working in the comfort of one's home. Neoliberalism finds this problematic because working in cyberspace is still centred around the acceleration of competition, regardless of flexible working locations. This is an example of how the widespread representations of modern lifestyles 'arise, develop, and are structured to shape a common social reality' (Moscovici, 2001, p. 110). This is significant because of the shift from liberalism to neoliberalism. As Beattie (2019, p.90) states, humans under liberalism 'were able to govern themselves, rather than by the best' or most privileged amongst them. Yet neoliberalism is problematic because flexible working locations allow individuals to develop within professional spheres whilst living out alternative lifestyles. In doing so, remote working has influenced people to leave cities and live in rural areas through the Covid-19 pandemic (Peachey, 2021). For example, the domestication of vehicles (which were not previously deemed as a 'home') have been adopted by climbers to enable flexible lifestyles. Individuals in this lifestyle, such as climbers, 'accept the compromise of infrastructural luxuries' (Oogjes et al., 2016, p.321) such as an unlimited hot water supply, large storage spaces, and central heating. Mobile lifestyles allow them to freely adapt to off-grid living styles whilst continuously travelling to different environments. This is significant to neoliberalism and rock-climbing because domesticised living space is capable of being mobile in Frykman and Lofgren's (1996) culture of stationary and secure communities. Mobile lives, therefore, share a relationship with flow because access to optimal experiences can be produced by disassociating oneself from competition-driven lifestyles. Further, an individual with this lifestyle is privileged with an additional period to gain more experience with flow and the body movements associated with climbing.

Engaging with activities that allow oneself to experience flow can revolutionise an individual's quality of life. This is because 'flow activities involve patterns of action which maximise immediate, intrinsic rewards to the participant' (Csikszentmihalyi, 1975, p.21). In this instance, climbing is useful because it involves challenge-setting and skill development, and the merging of action and awareness. Beck (1994) suggests that the impact of the global risk society and its inherent emphasis on risk in modern life has emphasised responsibility for one's own consequences in day-to-day life. In the urban and modernised western world, risk-taking has become a 'passive' experience alongside the survival of the physical body in everyday life. The physical body is often at risk whilst climbing because of the immediate danger associated with its participation. For example, traditional forms of climbing involve gear placement, when cams, nuts, and friends replace bolted protection on natural rock formations. Although 'risk' can be associated with danger and the physical body, Keinan and Bereby-Meyer (2012) suggest that 'risk' can occur during everyday life and through the concept of 'inaction inertia'. 'Inaction inertia' refers to people's tendency to act on the most favourable and safest option (Keinan and Bereby-Meyer, 2012, p.706), even though any action in everyday life still manifests risk. Examples of risk in everyday life include unexpected health issues, debt, harmful leisure activities, such as gambling, and the loss of paid work. Whilst everyday life carries some type of risk, climbing is significant because it is risk combined with sensation seeking, 'a trait defined by the seeking of varied, novel, complex, and intense sensations' (Zuckerman, 1994, p.27). The difference between 'everyday risk' and climbers' 'sensation-seeking risk' is that the climbers choose to experience risk which challenges their mortality. This is based on Llewellyn and Sanchez's (2008, p.423) observation that 'climbers take additional risks when motivated to develop a strong sense of mastery, to set themselves challenging goals and overcome their anxieties'. Climbers, and their relationship with mastery, is therefore connected with Csikszentmihalyi's (1975) flow because of the reward system associated with additional risk and the seeking of sensation. Outdoor rock-climbing influences people to take additional risks regardless of the constant exposure to risk in contemporary media, which challenges Keinan and Bereby's (2012) theory of inaction inertia. This is significant because risk societies do not hold some individuals back from placing their body in immediate risk.

Flow state is intrinsically connected with sensation seeking activities, such as extreme styles of rock climbing. Communities of climbers are therefore produced by a common group alignment of sensation seeking and competition, which drives individuals to engage with creative and difficult types of climbing, such as free soloing, traditional climbing, and strenuous bouldering. The competition element of communal climbing groups emerges from the drive to execute difficult climbing routes, which other members of these communities have previously completed. The term 'extreme' has been incorporated into popular media discourses, and it could be argued that it 'serves to co-opt any radical element of alternative sport' (Wheaton, 2000, cited by Robinson, 2008, p.2). This is significant because the discourse of 'extreme' is incorporated into leisure activities which do not align with safe and secure lives. Aside from rock-climbing, extreme leisure such as base jumping is outlawed in Yosemite National Park, the safest location to base jump in America (Branch, 2015). Base jumping shares a strong relationship with rock-climbing because of 'freebase', a style of climbing invented by Dean Potter. Freebase involves free soloing with a parachute to catch the climbers fall. Despite the measures which prohibit such activities, sensation seeking individuals will often carry out their practice at the safest venue regardless of legal authorities. This is problematic because base jumpers have been known to gamble their chance of survival and change their aerial route, risking and losing their lives to avoid park rangers in the Yosemite National Park (Carswell, 2015; Heywood, 2016). In this instance, the prohibition of extreme activities becomes problematic because risk avoidance can cause more risk for those who freebase. This is not to say that all climbers approve of extreme styles of rock-climbing, with some individuals requiring less sensation seeking experiences to reach an isolated state of flow. According to Csikszentmihalyi (2014, p.219), 'a central task of any human community is to make flow experience available to its members within productive, prosocial activities'. Risk taking shares a strong relationship with the values of communal climbing groups. In this instance, sport specific behaviours are intrinsically connected with one's rock-climbing social life. An increasing number of people have turned towards risk sports because the cultural norms of modern society impede individuals from living exciting, creative, autonomous, and liberated lives (Langseth and Salvesen, 2018). This is significant because the group alignment of sensation seeking climbers intensifies the values of extreme and risk-taking lifestyles. In doing so, the unique and strong emotions which individuals experience through climbing is shared with various members of climbing social groups.

Sensation seeking is influenced by an individual's unique experience of climbing media. This produces new and creative ways to practice outdoor climbing, usually involving higher intensity body moves and greater risk. This is often manifested in the form of traditional climbing, which is becoming more popular amongst online climbing media. Traditional climbing (also known as trad climbing) is a variation of hard bouldering moves and free soloing, due to the lack of protection placement on difficult climbing grades. Experienced climbers are naturally advantaged when it comes to their consumption of rock-climbing media. This is because their knowledge of specific techniques, climbing styles, and skills enable them to understand the process behind various practices included in climbing media. For example, the body techniques used on Alex Honnold's ascent of Free Rider create a profound experience for those with experience of intensive body movement in climbing. This is evidenced by Sherry (2004, p.344), who suggests that visual mediums 'require some training or experience order to have the skills necessary to read that medium, but those skills will differ amongst media'. Through the ability to read such experiences with depth, the climbing audience can connect with the characters within the sphere of climbing media, whilst developing their knowledge of rock climbing. This isn't to say that climbing media is exclusive, non-climbing audiences can also emotionally engage with climbing media, evidenced by the prolific success of Free Solo (2017). Emotional stimulation can be actively regulated by varying the strength and target of dispositional alignments based on the distance between characters and the self (Zillmann, 1994). Climbers are therefore more likely to engage with climbing media artefacts with more depth because they can compare themselves with various characters and athletes. By consuming climbing media and discovering new role models, individuals have been known to improve their relationship with the physical self (Hulya-Asci, 2004; Gleeson et al., 2017; Eldik et al., 2019). In doing so, individuals can compare their own physical bodies with elite climbers. There are both positive and negative aspects in the comparison of climbers and elite climbing athletes. For example, positive self-improvements and new training routes can be produced by athletic bodies. However, by associating climbing with muscle development and athletic bodies, the sport is being driven away from its focal point of technique and creativity. In doing so, the direction of rock-climbing is being influenced by the representation of the physical bodies through climbing media in cyberspace. This suggests that the representation of the self is intrinsically connected with climbing media. In this instance, strong physical bodies are required to experience sensation seeking activities.

Cyberspace shares an important relationship with climbing because of the representation of alternative outdoor lifestyles through rock-climbing vlogs. Vlogs (the visual equivalent of blogs) are designed to stimulate audiences' emotions through 'inspiration and escapism (Xu et al., 2021, p.1). Xu et al. (2021, p.1) suggest that it is unclear whether vlogs 'trigger positive perceptions' of travel destinations. Alongside this, Xu et al. (2021) assume that all leisure vlogs are used to commercialise travel destinations as a form of tourism. Rock-climbing vlogs are significant because they are also used as online guides for new and existing climbing venues, showing audiences how to climb routes and how to find them. A rock-climbing route is a combination of different rock shapes that create an overarching sequence that can be climbed by the human body. Climbing, therefore, allows these blank sheets of rock to become a site of body movement, hidden from the naked eye of walkers and tourists without access through vlogs and written guidebooks. Body movement and rock shapes share an important relationship with vlog tourism because they also challenge previous academic research on the behaviour and motivation of vlog audiences. Rock climbing and its relationship with vlogs is therefore more complex than the 'commercialisation' and appearance of travel destinations. This is because of the diverse set of needs which predispose a person to participate in tourist activity, now involve contemporary leisure activities such as rock climbing (Pizam et al., 1979). Chakravarty et al. (2021, p.2) contribute to this by suggesting that vlogs as a contemporary form of virtual travel 'enhance the quality of one's life by enabling participants to explore the unknown and share it with enthusiasm on screen'. Climbers take the enthusiasm from the screen and into their real-life practice by using climbing vlog locations as an outline for sites of body movement and leisure. In this instance, the audience of the climbing vlog can optionally use the knowledge shared in the vlog to produce and develop a rock-climbing lifestyle for themselves. Because of the distribution of such knowledge, the climbing audiences can actively engage and experience the lifestyles presented on contemporary rock-climbing vlogs, rather than isolated tourist consumption. This is significant because digital climbing videos stimulate a sense of adventure, improved physical appearance, and additional climbing knowledge.

In conclusion, this literature review has critically discussed how the consumption of rock-climbing media enables people to challenge normative ways of living. In doing so, climbing vlogs influence various life choices, such as physical risk in various climbing scenarios. Neoliberalism was used to suggest that risk and security as a deeply embedded cultural law prevents people from experiencing outdoor sports such as climbing. The chapter drew upon Foucault's (2008) concept of homo economicus to provide evidence that risk avoidance and security have become embedded behavioural norms. In this instance, the desire for freedom outside of cultural norms emerge from risk-taking as a voluntary choice. To further challenge the norms behind secure living styles, the chapter critically discussed Pinson and Journel's (2016) immobile neoliberal city. From this perspective, a secure life involves stationary and immobilised lives, which has been challenged through the emergence of a climber's relationship with 'van life' and travelling. The literature review emphasised the importance of traditional constraints to explain how cultural norms restrict people from experiencing mobilised climbing lifestyles. Alongside this, global transformations restrict individuals from various sports activities because of habitual identities and the division of social class. Csikszentmihalyi's (1990) theory of flow allowed the chapter to discuss how human consciousness is affected by the cultural and behavioural norms which originate from neoliberalism. This was said to impede on people's access to outdoor climbing, and its fulfilling relationship with flow state. This is significant because risk societies do not hold some individuals back from placing their bodies at immediate risk on outdoor climbing routes. The literature review then challenged the access of outdoor climbing by investigating how online climbing vlogs allow individuals to develop new and existing abilities through online learning. In doing so, online space has created the exposure of various and alternative lifestyles to a wider audience than a few privileged climbers. This is significant because vlog audiences are now able to develop experience and knowledge through digital media and use this to produce their own climbing lifestyle. Therefore, the consumption of rock-climbing media enables people to use climbing vlogs as a tool to escape from cultural and behavioural norms produced by neoliberalism.

Methodology

This chapter will discuss the methods used to explore how contemporary climbing vlogs are used as a cultural and informed learning tool. Videos of modern vlogs have been presented to participants during the interviews. Throughout this method, a qualitative approach has been taken to explore the recurring themes and ideas associated with the behaviours, learning methods, and flow in online climbing media. The chapter will then explain how the participants have been sampled. The data taken from the participants' answers has been organised into themes through the thematic analysis method, and further explored in chapter four; the findings and discussion chapter. An analysis of climbers' media consuming behaviour has also been produced to provide evidence that climbers recreate their own and unique climbing lifestyles through vlogs. This is carried out by learning about new techniques and potential climbing locations discovered in the content of climbing vlogs. The qualitative method and its relationship with climbing media have also been useful whilst developing various types, trends, and themes within the findings of the research project. The methodological approach of this study is made up of a semi-structured interview in combination with the video elicitation method. Part one of the methodology will explain how the semi-structured interview allowed the study to illustrate the participants unmediated perspectives of the climbing social world. In part two, the participants watched three climbing vlogs. The video elicitation method (Uhrig et al., 2016) was then used to develop a coherent understanding of the participants mediated perspectives of climbing media and its relationship with social norms and behaviours within spheres of rock-climbing communities. It is important to note that part one and two of the methodology are both a part of the same analysis. Part one and two have been used in this chapter to clearly outline the procedure of this methodological approach. I have purposively selected four climbing vlogs that provoke ideas about alternative lifestyles and behaviours outside of contemporary universal norms. In doing so, I chose vlogs that demonstrated a clear example of risk-taking in the context of the physical body. This is when Csikszentmilhalyi's (2014) 'non-thinking' is used as a method of psychological control when the body is positioned at a great height on a blank rock-face. In doing so, the sample vlogs have demonstrated that physical risk-taking is normalised in the day-to-day life of rock-climbing communities. Vlogs that challenge the adopted behaviours of safe and secure living include those created by Magnus Midtbo, Wide Boyz, Mellow, and Adam Ondra. Throughout the sampling strategy, I found various responses which incited different ideas about alternative behaviour and lifestyle choices within the rock-climbing social world. In doing so, the vlogs have been aligned with the video elicitation method to influence the participants to produce new and authentic ideas about rock-climbing communities and their relationship with digital media.

A Qualitative Approach

The qualitative research method (Silverman, 2020) has been used in this project to develop a coherent understanding of human behaviour within the online media activity of rock climbing. Rock-climbing media activity refers to the relationship between the content creators of climbing vlogs and their audiences. This relationship is significant because climbers are usually committed to active communities of practice (Wenger, 2011), which seek to engage with climbing media alongside group-based climbing activities. Through the literature review, I discovered that 'communities of practice are formed by people who engage in a process of collective learning in a shared domain of human endeavours' (Wenger, 2011, p.1). The concept of communities of practice shares an important relationship with this research project because human groups have become a primary focus within qualitative research. This is significant because a climber's individualised experience of behavioural norms within a wider social group is closely related to the emotions experienced through climbing vlogs. This allows qualitative methods to investigate the operations of behaviours, habits, and emotions in everyday human experience (Silverman, 2020). In doing so, this research project has investigated the lived experience of climbing audiences by developing a coherent understanding of the behaviours adopted by online vlog cultures. Agius (2018, p.204) also suggests that the qualitative method allows the researcher to 'gain an understanding of the experiences, perceptions or behaviours of those studied, and the meanings attached to them'. By using the qualitative method, the participants' readings of textual and visual media artefacts produced different inquiries on the behaviours which originate within climbing vlogs. This is significant because one of the core inquiries of this study sought the investigation of behaviour imitation, and its relationship with visual media artefacts.

Part one: Participants and climbing experience

Part one focuses on the participants unmediated responses to the interview questions. None of the participants were shown any media artefacts at the beginning of the interview. The term *unmediated* has been used to summarise that the participants' responses were offered prior to engaging with any media artefact before the video elicitation method in part two. In doing so, this allowed the study to illustrate the participants' unmediated perspectives and developed a coherent understanding of the participants' thoughts before the intervention of media artefacts. Eight national and international participants were recruited for this research project. They were made up of four men and four women, with a diverse age range from eighteen years old to sixty-five. The aim of the research project was to explore the consumer behaviour behind contemporary climbing vlogs. To ensure that the study contained useful and accurate data, the participants were required to have a reasonable understanding of climbing culture, both within media and real-life context. For the purpose of this study, an understanding of climbing culture involves at least three years' experience in the viewership of climbing vlogs, and weekly visits to indoor and outdoor climbing centres and venues. Anonymous members of local and international climbing communities alongside members of Team Great Britain's climbing team have been involved in this research project.

Participant Ethics

As the privacy of the participants is a priority in this study, they will all be made anonymous throughout this research project. In doing so, the method of this study will follow the guidelines of the Leeds Beckett University's Ethics Policy (2017, p.4). This ensures that the participants 'are not subjected to undue intrusion, distress, indignity, physical discomfort, personal embarrassment or other harm'. To further ensure confidentiality, the data produced throughout the course of the research project has been transcribed into words. The data included in the findings and discussion chapter has also been registered with false names to further protect the research projects participants from any harm. Alongside this, the project did not interview or gather data from vulnerable individuals. For this study, vulnerable individuals were classed as minors, or those with psychological disorders. Following the Leeds Beckett University's Ethics Policy (2017) was therefore prioritised to ensure that human participants were protected from any form of harm. Whilst this limited the number of participants involved in the study, the ideas shared by the participants with correct identification were still beneficial for this research project.

Recruitment

During the recruitment process, the research project used the snowball sampling method (Marcus et al., 2017) to increase awareness of the project at various local climbing walls. Alongside this, the research project was advertised on renowned climbing websites such as UKC and Camp to Camp. These are European blog hosts dedicated to the discussion of national and international climbing communities. Because the participants were all made up of national and international climbers, the advertisements posted on these websites played an important role in the recruitment process. In doing so, the recruitment method allowed the study to gather accurate and valuable information on the behavioural norms of various rock-climbing communities. The participants chosen showed enthusiasm for local climbing initiatives, demonstrated by the stories they shared about their climbing lives whilst agreeing to participate in the study. At this point, participant information sheets were handed over, alongside written and verbal consent from the participants. The interview stage was then carefully explained to them, stating that they could withdraw at any point of the study. Alongside this, it was explained that they would be made anonymous throughout the research project. After written consent was received from the participants, the research project then moved on to the data collection process. A limitation throughout the research project was the recruitment of diverse participants through online forums. This was a limitation because the online forums introduced a very wide sample of anonymous individuals. However, by using online space to find the participants, geographic challenges were resolved whilst also allowing participants from diverse backgrounds to be included in the study, producing accurate and rich data.

Data collection

The interviews were carried out in two ways: climb-along interviews and online zoom calls. In the context of Covid-19, the zoom calls were an important part of the data collection process to ensure the safety of vulnerable participants. The climb-along interview was based on Carpiano's (2009) 'walk-along' interview method. I adapted the walk-along method to fit the activity so they became 'climb-along', allowing climbing-relevant locations to influence the participants contribution to the research project. The interviews were carried out at The Climbing Lab, City Bloc, and popular outdoor climbing venues in West Yorkshire, the North of England, such as Almscliffe, Shipley Glen, and Crookrise. One-to-one semi-structured interviews were carried out to ensure that the study focused on the lived experience of all the participants. One-to-one semi-structured interviews enabled the participants to share their individualised experiences of rock-climbing vlogs and how they translate into real-life rock-climbing social groups. In doing so, semi-structured interviews, and their close relationship with interpretive sociology, allowed the study to investigate various media theory on self-interpretation and discursive understanding (see for example, Flick et al., 2004). There are however disadvantages to semi-structured interviews and the qualitative approach. For example, the interpretation of the participants' stories may have been recorded incorrectly (Flick et al., 2004). This could have been problematic because the participants' identity could have been revealed, and their personal stories could have been misinterpreted based on the researcher's perspective of their private data. To challenge this, the interviews were conducted as both face-to-face and online. Whilst online communication offers research participants the right to withdraw from an interview at any point (Janghorban et al., 2014), they can also be seen as problematic. This is because online interviews 'cannot capture the subtleties of body language and other social cues' (Smith and Sparkes, 2016, p.107). The benefits of online interviews include participants preferring communication with a researcher through the familiar and comfortable setting of online space (Salmons, 2014), whilst online interviews were more convenient for the participants and the researcher and therefore easier to arrange. However, it is arguably more difficult to build trust and rapport between the researcher and the participant in an online setting. In this instance, a face-to-face and intimate setting is needed to facilitate a space for empathy and trust (Smith and Sparkes, 2016). The climb-along interviews were designed for local participants in West Yorkshire and enabled the study to collect data about the participants' social lives whilst they were in a familiar space of socialisation and leisure. Climb-along interviews were face-to-face and took place at a local West Yorkshire climbing wall. Through the climb-along interview, the participants climbed whilst answering questions instead of using an online setting to carry out the interview. It is acknowledged that during the climb-along interviews participants are known to be more secretive about their acknowledged behavioural norms, due to being in a public space. By drawing on Goffman's (1990) front and back regions of the everyday self, I found that participants may have answered the questions with their front stage self in mind. This is based on Goffman's (1990, p.53) statement that the backstage self is 'defined as a place, relative to a given performance, where the impression fostered by performance is knowingly contradicted'. By acknowledging Goffman's (1990) representation of the everyday self, I was able to arrange the interviews around the behavioural norms adopted by climbing media. This allowed me to direct the study towards ideas and meanings produced in the internalised backstage self, alongside an individual's social and public performance. In doing so, the experience of everyday life can be integrated with one's perspective of climbing media by investigating how the behaviours found in digital space translate into real-life circumstances.

The interview process

The first ten minutes of all the interviews, both online and climb-along, consisted of an introductory conversation and an explanation of the study, and the signing of release forms. This was carried out to ensure that the participants were confident to move forward with the questioning. The participants were also reminded that they could withdraw from the study at any point and have their data deleted. In part one, I asked the participants different questions about risk, lifestyle, and about their overall thoughts on climbing vlogs. Fifteen minutes were then put aside to watch three different climbing vlogs. In part two, participants were then allocated fifteen minutes to watch three climbing vlogs. I then asked the participants if their perception of risk had changed since watching the vlogs and how this applied to their current climbing lifestyle. This allowed the study to a develop a mediated understanding of the participants attitudes, values, and behaviours in spheres of online and real-life climbing communities.

Part two: The Video Elicitation Method

The video elicitation method defines how pictures and videos can be used to investigate behavioural norms and emotions states without any type of deception (Uhrig et al, 2016). In doing so, the thematic analysis and video elicitation have both been used in this research project to produce accurate and valuable accounts of a climbers' experience of media consumption. This has been used to understand how the participants' experience of media translates into the social lives of rock-climbing communities. A rock-climbing social space refers to indoor rock-climbing gyms, and outdoor rock-climbing venues. These spaces allow groups of rock climbers to exchange ideas, knowledge, and behaviours taken from their personalised media consuming habits. According to Dencker-Larsen and Lundberg (2016, p.4) images and videos 'directly and indirectly, channel discourses on how the viewer should behave, look, and lead his or her life'. The media which climbers consume may determine the social behaviour that they take into rock-climbing space. This is significant because online climbing vlogs carry behavioural repertoires which introduce climbing audiences into new and exciting environments. For example, Orth (et al., 2018) has recorded how the development of skill in rock-climbing involves destabilising and reorganising of new behaviours. This expands the boundaries of an individual's competence and gives them access to explore new and exciting climbing environments. In doing so, climbing vlogs were a crucial part of this research method, justified by their ability to incite new meanings into rock-climbing environments. To justify my methodological approach, I have used the video elicitation method to demonstrate that qualitative research challenges contemporary academic understandings of social behaviour. This provided evidence that one-to-one interviews contribute towards the delivery of a clear and coherent explanation of climbing communities, and how they interact with climbing vlogs.

Thematic Analysis

To successfully measure the relationship between one's climbing social life and its relationship with climbing vlogs, a thematic analysis was produced from the personal stories shared by the study's participants. According to Finlay (2021, p.103) 'thematic analysis is a qualitative research method that aims to identify patterns and meanings within data'. The highlights taken from the interview participants' personal stories were divided into three foundational themes, produced by the intervention of online climbing vlogs. These themes were then applied to relevant theoretical literature on social behaviour, media theory, and consuming habits. All the themes and theoretical literature included in the study were combined with the participants' experiences of rock-climbing. This was carried out to produce a research project with fair and accurate perspectives outside of my internal viewpoint of rock-climbing media and social behaviour. According to Maguire et al. (2017, p.3351) the qualitative researcher uses thematic analysis to 'understand, describe and interpret experiences and perceptions'. Throughout the study, the video elicitation method reminded the participants about their personal experiences in communities of rock-climbers. By applying academic literature to these stories, and formatting them into various themes, the study was able to establish the relationship between climbers, and their underlying attachment to the behaviours in climbing vlogs. This was carried out by identifying the features of the participants' answers, and classifying them into units of meaning, which were then coded into recurring patterns of mediated behaviours adopted by various media (Guest et al., 2011).

Conclusion

This chapter has discussed the methods which have been used to explore how contemporary climbing vlogs influence social behaviour and produce online spaces of community learning. Videos of modern vlogs were presented to participants halfway through the interviews to investigate the unmediated and mediated answers before and after the influence of climbing media. Throughout this chapter, the qualitative method and its useful relationship with climbing media analysis has been mentioned to justify the study's chosen methodological approach. This has allowed the study to develop various types, trends, and themes for the findings of this research project. The qualitative research method has been used to analyse the recurring themes and ideas which emerged from the behaviours, values, and use of flow in online climbing media. The chapter also explained how the participants were sampled to justify that age and gender diversity has been incorporated into the methodology. From this, the data taken from the participants' answers has been organised into themes using the thematic analysis method, ready for further analysis in chapter four: Findings and Discussion.

Findings and discussion

This chapter will discuss the qualitative data taken from the interviews outlined in the methods chapter. To analyse the qualitative data, academic literature has been applied to the participants' social experience of rock-climbing. The chapter will organise the findings into different themes to ensure that the study's main arguments are clearly grouped together. This will ensure that the reader is able to digest the study's findings and assess the relationship between climbing and modern media text. The social experiences of the study's participants will be investigated through the readings taken from the previous chapter forming the literature review. Throughout, the chapter will draw on Beck's (1991) reading of risk, Foucault's (2008) perspective of neoliberalism, and Csikszentmihalyi's (1990) concept of flow. Through this, the participants will provide evidence that media text influences people to idolise and imitate 'correct' and 'appropriate' rock-climbing behaviours. However, it is also important to consider that the participants rejected modern media ideals projected by contemporary climbing vlogs. In doing so, theme one will suggest that social connections allow climbers to pursue advanced climbing development. However, it is important to note that an individual's involvement in niche climbing communities is a social privilege. Theme two outlines how the development of online climbing vlogs are capable of challenging contemporary climbing norms and behaviours. Theme three will challenge the inclusive nature of online rock-climbing by investigating elite behaviour types found in British rock-climbing social groups. This will reveal that 'showing no fear', 'machoism', and 'self-interest' have become embedded into the wider context of the modern climbing culture.

Theme 1: Risk

The theme of risk explored how international climbing vlogs influenced the knowledge shared amongst West Yorkshire climbing communities. This introduced behaviours associated with managing various emotional processes which emerge from climbing moves whilst free-soloing. In doing so, this shared a significant relationship with climbing media because the participants showed a clear interest in the ability of professional climbers in online climbing vlogs. Magnus Midtbo's and Adam Ondra's vlogs displayed a consistent demonstration of definitive focus whilst engaging in the movement of rock-climbing. Max (anonymised through pseudonym as per all participants) suggested that the feeling of motivation destabilises the invasion of anxious feelings which arise during dangerous climbing routes. Further, Max put a clear emphasis on the organisation of one's thoughts, and how all other stressful components of life must be put away to climb successfully:

> *I feel a lot of anxiety whilst climbing high-risk routes, such as free-soloing, or when my body is at physical risk. However, I usually put my energy into focusing on each move to put my mind off that. Why do I climb in risky scenarios? To feel a sense of relief when I reach the top and like I have achieved something.*

The anxiety that individuals experience whilst climbing is significant because of the diverse ways that emotional releases are conveyed between different climbers. Emotional release is a primary component of self-improvement within extreme styles of climbing. Climbing styles such as alpine, soloing, and traditional climbing can only be carried out by managing one's anxieties whilst the body is at physical risk. Scott (2021, p.1) argues that 'the emotions experienced within sport are the defining characteristic in explaining its prominence within various lives'. In this instance, the most important aspect of climbing becomes about managing and improving one's individualised set of emotional characteristics, rather than the climbing itself. Further, Max suggested that overcoming anxiety is central to a climber's ambition within the sphere of extreme styles of climbing. In doing so, this suggests that elite climbers express themselves in diverse ways whilst performing at their maximum physical and mental ability within risk-induced scenarios. For example, Alex Honnold's methodical and static style seen in his ascent of The Shining Path (2014) is naturally opposed to Ondra's dynamic movement with power screaming in Silence (2018). Although climbers convey their emotions in diverse ways whilst climbing, the findings show that individualised emotional releases are a coping mechanism for overcoming fear and anxiety. Garrido-Palomino and Espana-Romero (2019, p.285) draw on the concept of 'information processing efficiency' to suggest that 'anxiety may play a different role for some climbers, producing an improvement in their performance'. Garrido-Palomino and Espana-Romero (2019) have used the concept of information processing efficiency (IPE) to suggest that anxiety and clear thinking share a balanced relationship. IPE and its relationship with various sports are based on the phenomenon that people who exercise regularly have clearer thoughts in their day-to-day lives (Beckham Blomquist and Danner, 1987). The findings of this study show that information processing efficiency does not directly apply to extreme styles of climbing. This is because extreme styles of climbing are centred around the management of one's individualised anxiety, rather than repressing the characteristics of emotional turbulence during physical risk. Contrary to this, feelings of pre-performance anxiety can be used as a tool to improve one's performance. Pre-performance anxiety occurs before an individual engages in a sports-based activity. This commonly occurs in different styles of route climbing and other various extreme and non-extreme sports. In doing so, Sanchez et al.'s (2010) paper on climbing performance suggests that successful climbers show higher levels of pre-performance anxiety on difficult routes, in comparison to their unsuccessful counterparts. However, for some climbers, free-soloing can be viewed as a soothing experience, rather than an anxiety-provoking exercise. One of the study's participants, Asha, suggested that relying on various climbing techniques has allowed him to enjoy different elements of free-soloing without fear or anxiety:

> *You've got to rely on all the technique you have learnt over the years when it comes to soloing, that's when it all comes into play. However, I like to solo for an enjoyable experience, knowing all the holds is loads more fun than doing a harder route. For example, I watched Dave McLeod solo an 8b+ on one of his vlogs. That will never be for me, and that level of high risk does not appeal to me that much.*

The body technique associated with climbing and flow is intrinsically connected because of their relationship with non-thinking and problem-solving. Body technique is a phrase that refers to the motion that the body uses to navigate itself through various climbing routes. In this instance, the physical motion of the body can be seen as an 'expression of existing social conditions which determine how people perceive and control their physical selves' (Heinemann, 1980, p.41). Asha suggested that the success of free-soloing is made possible through years of physical processes which gradually change the physical appearance of the body. This suggests that a strong mind and physical body facilitate a 'safe' free-soloing experience. The significance of 'safe' free-soloing comes from the changing meaning of risk and safety within social spheres of rock-climbing communities. Heywood (2006, p.456) suggests that 'high-risk climbing involves exacting physical and mental preparation, considerable knowledge, and a careful calculation of the odds'. Through extreme styles of rock-climbing, it is clear that individuals are given the opportunity to govern themselves and their own bodies. In this instance, members of modern society are granted access to their private ownership of self-reflexivity and production. However, the sample of this study did not consider risk as an essential part of extreme climbing. For participants, risk in an immediate sense of danger was not included in the act of free-soloing itself. The participants did however emphasise the chance of risk when it came to the capability of a climber's body and mind. For example, one of the study's participants, Zoe, compared the risk of free-soloing with normalised practices which are carried out by modern citizens in everyday life. She suggested that a robust memory of a route, alongside the correct physical training and preparation, can produce a safe environment for free-soloing:

Climbing is no riskier than anything else you do. Risk is a multiplication of the likelihood of something going wrong and the consequence of when it does go wrong. For example, the consequence of crashing your car on the motorway is high, but the likelihood of it happening is very low. This means that the risk of a professional climber free-soloing is actually very low. However, for a beginner climber trying out climbing in a safe indoor environment, the risk is actually higher for them.

Conroy and Gonzalez (2017) have used the concept of the 'copycat phenomenon' to argue that scholars such as Herrera (2002) suggest that climbing media influences wider cultural audiences to participate in unsafe climbing practices. 'Highly publicised free-solos can lead others to copy that behaviour, leading people into risky situations with which they are not prepared to deal' (Conroy and Gonzalex, 2017, p.70). For Herrera (2002), a society that abides by the nature of freely chosen risks can lead to dangerous behaviours. For the participants in this study, risk-induced climbing practices were centred around preparation, goal setting, and patience. However, the participants of this study suggested that risk-induced styles of climbing are comparable with the usual and non-threatening risks involved in everyday life. Rock climbing's strong association with injury and death (Raunch et al., 2019) suggests that climbers have an alternative relationship with climbing media. For example, the participants in this study felt desensitised towards images of risk-taking behaviours. This is also evidenced by Russell (2005, p.16) who suggests that 'dangerous sport does not have anything like social costs; its costs by and large fall on the participants themselves'. Although individualisation shares a strong relationship with extreme sports and climbing, a climber's social life can affect and impact upon their athletic performance. This is because free-solo climbers do not necessarily climb in isolation and must consider those around them, such as fellow climbers, friends, and walkers (Conroy and Blunt-Gonzalez, 2017). Alongside this, free-soloing has been recorded as having strong positive personal values which share no relationship with the adulation of specific audiences. Individualisation in rock-climbing cultures refers to the 'beliefs, attitudes, and behaviours that are increasingly based on decisions of a personal nature and depend less on tradition' (Llopis-Goig, 2016, p.152). By disengaging with traditional values, it is clear that the personalised nature of decision-making has influenced climbers to engage with risk-induced styles of rock-climbing. However, the participants in this study showed a competitive interest in their climbing peers through the observation of digital videos showcasing their completed climbing routes, as stated by Asha:

Climbing is more than 'just a sport to me now', it's

> *my lifestyle. Vlogs do play a role in mirroring this experience to people who have never tried it. By sharing the same objectives as other climbers, taking the same risks, and climbing the same routes as them, it gives us a reason to stay in touch and continue working together. Unless I progress further than them, or our priorities in life change.*

This suggests that the social life which surrounds climbing is being merged with digitalised videos, vlogs, and online space as well as real-life encounters. In this instance, the emergence of risk as a personal choice shares a strong relationship with climbing social spheres. This is because risk is being reconstructed into a cultural and collective experience through climbing vlogs, various climbing media, and climbing communities. This is evidenced by West and Allin (2010, p.1235) who suggest that 'the motivation for lifestyle-sport participation has been linked to friendship and self-efficacy'. In this instance, climbing communities use climbing vlogs to develop their knowledge on new types of climbing language, climbing routes, and role models. This is significant because local friendships are developed through the shared achievement of local outdoor climbing routes, which the participants stated they found through online vlogs.

In conclusion, the distribution of climbing knowledge within West Yorkshire climbing groups provided evidence that social connections allow climbers to pursue development in their climbing goals without professional coaching. However, being involved in a niche climbing community is a social privilege, which challenges how various individuals find access to communities of learning.

Theme Two: Media Intimacy

The theme of mediatised intimacy explores how the participants used vlogs to develop co-present relationships with their favourite climbing athletes. The findings showed that the participants' social behaviours were produced by one-way online relationships with climbing role models. Social behaviours are produced by social norms, a 'cultural phenomena that prescribe and proscribe behaviour in specific circumstances' (Hechter and Opp, 2001: xi). One-way relationships refer to the way that media audiences develop copresence with online role models, through online vlogs. The participants stated that the way they communicated with the online role models was primarily text-based through the comments section on YouTube. This revealed that online role models respond to their audience by producing a universal message for their audiences in their following videos. For example, Dave Macleod (2020) has created a beginner's introduction to trad climbing and free-soloing in response to his audience's messages about improving their outdoor climbing. This suggests that climbing audiences do not usually share an interpersonal relationship with online role models. However, they do receive a shared message in response to their collective understanding of rock-climbing-related content with other climbing audiences. This supports Berlant's (2008) understanding of real-life intimacy, challenging how climbing audiences implement digital behaviours into real-life social interactions. 'Intimacy' in a digital context refers to the relationship which audiences form with online role models. Berlant's (2008) work on intimacy is significant because it illustrates the divergent characteristics of digital and real-life behaviours. In doing so, Berlant (2008) suggests that 'intimacy builds worlds; it creates spaces and usurps places meant for other kinds of relations'. Real-life communication contains verbal and nonverbal symbols and signs that are influenced by social interactions between different people. This is also evidenced by Heider (1958, p.1), who suggests that 'a person reacts to what he/she thinks the other person is perceiving, feeling, and thinking, in addition to what the other person may be doing'. From this perspective, the one-way structure of audiences and YouTube vloggers do not enable climbing audiences to immerse themselves in digital learning and social practices. One of the study's participants, Eleanor, suggested that digital communication and climbing vlogs are limited because they do not offer people realistic social scenarios:

Reminiscing through old climbing vlogs during lockdown helped me get through a lot, but because I wasn't with the vloggers, or climbing with them in their physical space, I couldn't satisfy my curiosity

> *by asking them about different rope techniques and difficult climbing moves. Besides this, coming out of lockdown made me realise how important it is to be around other climbers and engage with them. It's impossible to make the impossible climb possible without a solid real-life climbing partner who supports your goals, that is a fact.*

For Eleanor, learning through digital videos lacks practice and meaning when it comes to rock-climbing. This is significant because Luckin and Weatherby (2014) draw on Wenger's (1998) communities of practice to suggest that online space contributes towards an individual's development in the real world. Online spaces are embodied by textual discussion, which are produced by various communities. Rock-climbing space includes the discussion on access to local crags, recent climbing ascents, and the effectiveness of contemporary training routines. This is significant because these discussions can be found across a broad range of online climbing spaces, for example, the comments section of online vlogs, forums such as UKC, and through the social media channels of popular climbing role models. According to Luckin and Weatherby (2014, p.7), 'a learner's activity as part of an online learning community might be connected to their relationships and collaborations both within and beyond that online community'. From this perspective, online space can help individuals develop themselves, and they can use the knowledge found in these spaces during face-to-face discussions with other climbers. This is based on the understanding that 'groups of people [are] informally bound together by shared expertise and passion for a joint enterprise' (Wenger and Snyder, 2000, p.139). Eleanor suggested that she was not interested in the online communities because of their elitist behaviours, unlike the real-life connections she has made with rock-climbing communities. Some of the participants in this study were made up of individuals currently performing above average on the bouldering grading system. Therefore, it is important to consider that those climbing within an inclusive grade bracket are associated with social circles which are viewed as 'elite'. Through the UK Climbing Forum (UKC, 2003), it is clear that elite attitudes and values have become associated with people climbing at an advanced level. According to Rokeach (1973, p.5), values are an 'enduring belief that a specific mode of conduct or end-state of existence is personally or socially preferable to an opposite or converse mode of conduct or end-state of existence'. In doing so, values that are found within elite climbing social groups have acquired behaviours that they resort to over 'alternative behaviours' outside of their social group. An elite climbing social group refers to a category of climbers who have attained a superior fitness level, which is showcased in their rock-climbing achievements. In doing so, the term 'alternative behaviour' has been used to describe various climbing methods which overlook practices involving pressure and their relationship with success. However, pressure and its relationship with rock-climbing are complicated because of the diverse range of climbing styles and terrain. For example, climbers feel an increased amount of 'time pressure during a lead climb and rated their performance as being better during top rope roping (Draper et al., 2010 p.17). It is also important to consider that the practice of climbing involves a disproportionate rise in an individual's heart rate (Draper et al., 2010). According to Draper et al. (2010), it is important to consider the overall physiological demands of climbing whilst interpreting the participants' data, regardless of their chosen climbing style. One of the study's participants, Alex, mentioned that their climbing style does not align with pressure because it produces an increased sense of fear:

> *In some of the climbing videos I watch, there's a huge theme surrounding the flash attempt. A flash attempt is when you climb a route in one, the first time, without any mistakes. For me, this is fun to watch in terms of my online climbing life, but I don't enjoy practicing this style of climbing. For my climbing, I perform at my very best without external pressure, without feeling let down if I don't get my flash attempt, I want to take as long as I want and get my very best attempt down. This is important because a lot of my peers are content with getting the flash attempt, and competing for it with each other, it's all about getting the first prize. For me, this doesn't matter so much, I want to encourage my friends and have a great time whilst trying hard.*

Pressure and its relationship with rock-climbing refer to intensive styles of rock-climbing such as soloing and flash attempting a climbing route. This is significant because flash attempts associate the notion of pressure into the social life of rock-climbing. In doing so, digital media shapes social reality, and flash attempts found on online climbing vlogs translate into the routine of a climber's social experience. This is correlated with McLuhan's (1964) understanding that contemporary digital technology is an extension of the self. Further, the personal and social consequences 'of any extension of ourselves result from the new scale that is introduced into our affairs by each extension of ourselves, or by any new technology' (McLuhan, 1964, p.1). This suggests that the extension of the technological and digital self has introduced social pressure into rock-climbing through normative behaviours found on climbing vlogs. For example, the participants in this study suggested that their outdoor climbing objectives and projects were guided by their peer's activity on Instagram reels and by renowned climbers on YouTube. Through this, the 'Instagram effect' of rock-climbing disguises the banal and ordinary elements of British climbing - which involves hours spent in the cold and falling off a climbing route several times over. In this instance, the competitive aspect of outdoor rock-climbing is directed by online activity. LaRose et al. (2014) suggests that online connections lead to negative consequences and habits. Rock-climbing, however, demonstrates that online activity allows people to immerse themselves in new and exciting aspirations through their online connections with other climbers. The positive aspect of relationships and connections in online spheres of rock-climbing are also centred on the distribution of new and exciting rock-climbing lines. These locations were previously confidential and only shared between specific social groups because of the elite nature of the sport (Robinson, 1985). This is also evidenced by Wenger (1998, p.52), who suggests that 'our engagement with practice may have patterns, but it is the production of such patterns anew that give rise to an experience of meaning'. Although online connections allow for the distribution of knowledge, the behavioural patterns of elite climbing groups perhaps produce environments where knowledge is not being shared with novices. It is important to note that these behaviours have become embedded into outdoor rock-climbing social norms. Original media artefacts, such as The Real Thing (1996) and Statement of Youth (1984) influence patterns of learning which affect the elite nature of outdoor rock-climbing. By drawing on Alex's experience of rock-climbing, those within elite climbing groups are becoming aware of behavioural patterns which do not apply to their unique values. In doing so, this demonstrates that the awareness of elite behaviour is being acknowledged because more people are exposing themselves to difficult climbing and the social life accompanied by it.

In conclusion, the development of online communication has produced an inclusive nature that challenges contemporary climbing norms and behaviours. Whilst this is partly because of the internet's natural distribution of knowledge and information, climbing vlogs play an imperative role by showing a wide variety of behaviours to climbing audiences. In doing so, audiences are exposed to behaviours found in interpersonal climbing friendships and relationships, where encouragement and support become the most important aspect of an individual's climbing experience.

Theme 3: Social Regulation

The theme of individualised societies focused on the climbers' relationship with the cultural experience of rock-climbing communities. In doing so, the participants suggested that the practice of climbing itself is an immersive and individualised experience, separate from their social life in rock-climbing. Through Csikszentmihalyi's (1990) Flow, individuals experience states of concentration whilst carrying out challenging activities such as rock-climbing. However, Csikszentmihalyi (2014) suggests that communities are essential in flow state, which makes the experience of flow available to more people. Thus, 'a central task of any human community is to make flow experience available to its members within productive, prosocial activities' (Csikszentmihalyi, 2014, p.219). Although learning has a strong relationship with an individual's social life (Field, 2004), rock-climbing is centered around individualisation. The stimulus field of rock-climbing itself is consumed by an individualised and immersive experience, despite the accompaniment of belayers or spotters. For example, the balance between a difficult task and time pressure leads to flow state Csikszenmihalyi (1997). During the immersive experience of rock-climbing, 'the sense of duration of time is altered: hours pass by in minutes, and minutes can stretch out to seem like hours' (Csikszenmihalyi, 1997, p.49). Although the practical experience of rock-climbing is individualised, the culture of rock-climbing produces social rituals which mobilise climbers into the same space (Cailly, 2006). The ritual is carried out by investigating effective climbing styles whilst engaging with various climbing routes and discussing historical artefacts related to rock-climbing venues. Once climbers find peers who are encouraged by graded climbing, they are given the opportunity to form relationships centered around competition. Climbing grades are significant because the element of competition is now intrinsically connected to agencies of recreation. Competition is now manifested into relationships with other people, and the self. One of the study's participants, Marian, suggested that people produce their impression of rock-climbing cultures based on their previous social experiences in climbing space:

I once experienced some online grief for a climbing video that I posted on an online forum, just because my beta was different from everyone else's. Some climbers have always been guilty of trying to take away achievements from other people. For example, various local first ascents have had all sorts of fuss because the person who climbed it in the first place wasn't a 'local'. However, I am often guilty of the competitive edge that climbing brings to the table, it's inherent in our human nature. I find myself competing with myself, and other people. Obviously, this style of competition requires everyone to work as a team, we help each other get the route! But, if one of my friends gets it, I need to get it too. That's the great thing about vlogs though, they're showing positive behaviours by being great role models. I've never seen Magnus or Macleod put anyone down, they just share their passion for the sport, making it a welcoming place for everyone.

By drawing on Eleanor's experience of online and real-life climbing social experiences, the cultural behaviour of recreational risk sports such as rock climbing is driven by competition. In this instance, it is important to consider the influence of role models in online and real-life encounters. Much like popular cultures, climbing vloggers are perceived as micro-celebrities in rock-climbing cultures, therefore playing an important role as media idols (Gleason et al., 2017). However, the influence of popular media identities does not determine the behaviour of people who Eleanor has encountered in her climbing social life. In doing so, the behaviours found in climbing space share an equal role in the development of rock-climbing cultures, as well as online climbing media such as vlogs. Eldik et al.'s (2019) concept that media idols influence contemporary social behaviours can now be challenged through the development of diverse social norms in both online and real-life contexts. It is also important to consider the emergence of 'risk-taking' in western societies (Bunn, 2017). In doing so, 'a participant's level of engagement in an activity is related to the intrinsic or extrinsic motivations' (Grant et al., 2013, p.34). This suggests that individuals engage with the practice of climbing to resist contemporary restrictions created by ideals such as neoliberalism. In this instance, individuals respond to neoliberal restrictions through the participation of extreme outdoor recreation. This is significant because rock-climbing lifestyles are naturally inseparable from powerful and intensive social behaviours in response to contemporary restrictions. By drawing on the work of Beattie (2019), for example, people were able to govern themselves before the rise of neoliberal social values. Therefore, to immerse oneself in the lifestyle of outdoor rock-climbing, the climber may find themselves resisting traditional norms in a neoliberal context. However, it is also important to consider that neoliberal values produce individualised social norms. In doing so, the economy is capable of dividing people into different spheres of living. Through this, neoliberalism shares a relationship with one's self-identity through power relations

(McDonald et al., 2017). Although some of the outdoor climbers in this study have disembodied themselves from consumer-based lifestyles, power relations are still capable of regulating their self-identification with others. One of the study's participants, Alistair, suggested that British climbers are programmed differently from European and Asian climbers. Further, he also suggested that British climbers are known for enforcing 'extreme values' and pushing out the 'fun and innocence of climbing':

> *Sport climbers are notorious for enforcing extreme ethics into climbing, innocent people get involved, so do entire countries. It's alright if we go over to Spain or India to bolt a new venue, yet if anyone from outside of the UK came over to here and did that to us, we'd of course be unhappy about it. Is this a safe and friendly environment for new climbers? I don't think so. Thankfully, I've noticed that climbing vlogs are representing the positive side of climbing. Vloggers like Magnus allow new people to get into more inclusive types of climbing by making the viewer feel a part of their journey, they're not even afraid to show they get scared on a route, which has become a stigma in climbing. This way, people watch the highs and lows which come with the experience of climbing, they relate to these emotions, and feel more involved.*

The 'elite nature' of rock-climbing's social politics influences climbing groups to embody the notion of hierarchical competence as a social norm within climbing spaces. This is significant because 'fear' has become stigmatised in various rock-climbing communities. Tyler's (2020) perspective of stigma shares a direct relationship with power, rather than social interactions inside and within human groups (Goffman, 1963). However, for this study, stigma refers to membership which individuals acquire to attach themselves to groups of equivalence inside the cultural experience of rock-climbing. According to Goffman (1963, p.12), stigma refers to an attribute that 'stigmatises one type of possessor to confirm the unusualness of another'. In doing so, climbing's classic association with machoism and competence (Erickson, 1975) hinders the opportunity to develop for many people. Exposure to fear is experienced by performing difficult climbing moves above protection. In doing so, exposing a climber to their own fears is a fundamental part of developing rock-climbing ability. Therefore, the machoistic social act of 'showing no fear' prevents climbers from improving their abilities. This is because they are more likely to avoid rock-climbing scenarios which reveal their relationship with fear. Fear shares an important relationship with competence and ability in the spheres of rock-climbing communities. Groups of climbers with equivalent competence are now capable of governing power relations between local climbing groups and international communities. In some cases, minority groups are being excluded from producing an independent rock-climbing culture. Whilst defending the climbing rights of international countries, Alistair stated that he'd experienced conflict whilst asking his peers to avoid bolting new climbing routes in other countries. This is synonymous of British imperialism, because of course, the United Kingdom governed countries such as India in 1858, disrupting their potential to develop as an independent country (O'Dwyer, 2016). Kilvington (2013) has used other sports such as football to explore how minority groups are being unfairly excluded from modern practices. Though rock-climbing communities accommodate an 'impartial' exterior, it is important to consider the 'colourblind rhetoric' of climbing, and its relationship with neoliberal values. Mascarenhas (2012) has investigated how privileged individuals celebrate their virtues whilst blaming nations and various identities for their incompetence. In this instance, neoliberalism influences climbers to behave pro-socially with people inside of their inclusive social circles whilst excluding others. According to Foucault (2008, p.226), 'in neo-liberalism, the homo economicus is an entrepreneur of himself... being for himself his own capital, being for himself his own producer'. Through this, some climbers are still immersed in the neoliberal frame of mind, despite their resistance from risk-averse societies. The neoliberal mindset produces a cultural dynamic that affects individuals from all types of backgrounds. Therefore, rock-climbing, and its relationship with competition and flow state has produced a strict behavioural environment that once sought to resist Beck's (1991) risk-free society. This is significant because the desire for freedom has produced a community that is now moderated with rules, regulations, and norms. In doing so, the cultural dynamic of competition, and the appropriation of international climbing cultures is synonymous with the society that rock-climbing aimed to resist.

In conclusion, the emergence of new behaviours in rock-climbing social spheres arises from immersed and individualised climbing experiences as well as the consumption of online climbing media. By investigating the 'elite nature' of rock-climbing social groups, it is clear that 'showing fear' has become stigmatised and embedded into the wider context of the modern climbing culture. This revealed that groups of experienced climbers celebrate their virtues whilst excluding international climbing communities. Therefore, by producing routes in countries outside of the United Kingdom, it is clear that the elite nature of British climbing extends beyond social circles and into notions of imperialism and neoliberalism.

Conclusion

Chapter one, the literature review suggested that outdoor rock-climbing enables people to challenge normative ways of living through the experience of risk. The chapter used three key writers to investigate flow theory's relevance to risk-taking in contemporary rock-climbing media. Foucault's (2008) perspective of neoliberalism outlined the significance of individualised entrepreneurship, and how it affects people's instinctive human nature. Beck's (2014) risk-free society was then applied to suggest that risky leisure pursuits have become more attractive because of the enforcement of safe and ordinary lives within neoliberal governance. Social norms were included in the chapter to investigate how outdoor climbing lifestyles are restricted in popular consumer cultures through the construction of 'acceptable' behaviour (McDonald et al., 2017). In doing so, Csikszentmihalyi's (1990) theory of flow allowed the chapter to discuss how human consciousness is affected by the cultural and behavioural norms which originate from neoliberalism.

The chapter investigated flow and its relevance to risk-taking in contemporary rock-climbing media through climbing vlogs and their relevance to rock-climbing consumer audiences. From this perspective, the chapter was able to identify how climbing media is used to escape from cultural and behavioural norms produced by neoliberal governance. It is important to consider that neoliberal governance directs contemporary social norms through deeply embedded competition and collective organisation (Read, 2009; Beattie, 2019). Foucault's (2008) reading on homo-economicus was then challenged by suggesting that human activity is organised and controlled through individualised entrepreneurship (Beck, 2014). This is significant because the notion of 'risk' has become central within governed societies (Beck, 1991). Through this, the desire for freedom emerges from a modernised and industrial world centered around economics, individualised security, and the pursuit of self-interest. It is through climbing vlogs that wider audiences are given the opportunity to expose themselves to alternative climbing lifestyles that were formerly granted for the privileged few. According to neoliberalism, modern life prevents individuals from experiencing Csikszentmihalyi's (1990) Flow. This reveals that some individuals engage with the experience of flow by resisting risk-averse lifestyles through risk cultures such as rock-climbing.

In doing so, rock-climbing vlogs produce access to knowledge of outdoor rock climbing. In return, rock-climbing audiences are given the opportunity to engage with flow state, which is characterised by the mental and physical demands of outdoor rock-climbing.

Chapter Two: Methodology

Chapter two, the methodology section, discussed the methods used to investigate climbing vlogs and their purpose as a cultural and informed learning tool. The method of this study included video elicitation in cooperation with 'climb-along' interviews. The chapter then explained how the qualitative research method was used to develop recurring themes and ideas. These themes were used in the findings and discussion chapter to analyse the emergence of contemporary social behaviour in rock-climbing vlogs.

The analysis included climbers' media-consuming behaviour, and provided evidence that climbers recreate their own unique climbing lifestyles, envisioned through climbing vlogs. 'Climb-along' interviews illustrated the sensory experience of fear by discussing the participants' personal experiences in locations of recreational climbing practice. The individualistic responses from the climb-along interviews investigated the 'real-life' and mediated understanding of social behaviour in rock-climbing communities. This investigation was carried out by separating the interview into two halves. The first half examined the participants' overall thoughts about rock-climbing vlogs and the lifestyle of rock-climbing cultures. This was followed by watching three climbing vlogs created by Magnus Midtbo, Adam Ondra, and Anna Hazlenutt. The second half of the interview observed how the participant's perception of risk had changed since watching the vlogs, and how this related to each climber's individualised climbing lifestyle. The study also ensured that age and gender diversity were incorporated into the methodology by following a coherent sampling strategy.

In doing so, the chapter discussed the methods which were used to explore how contemporary climbing vlogs influence mediated social behaviours and produce online spaces of cultural learning. Further, the qualitative method was used to justify the study's chosen methodological approach. This enabled the study to develop various types, trends, and themes related to social behaviour and rock-climbing media for chapter three, the findings and discussion chapter.

Chapter three: Findings and Discussion

Chapter three, the findings and discussion chapter discussed the qualitative data found during the 'climb-along' interviews. The chapter organised the qualitative findings into three different themes to ensure that the study's key points were correctly and clearly organised. Organising the findings into themes also ensured that the study was able to clearly assess the relationship between rock-climbing and modern media text. The findings and discussion chapter consistently referred to the academic material found in chapter two, the literature review. This was carried out to ensure that neoliberalism

(Foucault, 2008), risk (Beck, 1991), and flow (Csikszentmihalyi, 1990) were embedded into the study's main discussion.

Risk

Through social connections, the theme of risk suggested that climbers develop their repertoire of climbing experience through their commitment to various rock-climbing communities. This suggested that the comments section of climbing vlogs creates effortless access to online rock-climbing communities. However, to immerse oneself into a real-life rock-climbing community requires years of commitment. This theme suggested that risk is reconstructed into a cultural and collective experience through climbing vlogs and media artefacts. The emotions experienced within a specific sport are intrinsically connected to an individual's social behaviour (Scott, 2021). In doing so, fear shares a strong relationship with individualisation because of the inclusive nature of rock-climbing, which shares a direct relationship with one's social behaviour.

Media intimacy

The theme of media intimacy suggested that the development of online communication is encouraging an inclusive environment for rock-climbing. Intimacy in the form of one-way online relationships challenges contemporary climbing norms through the vlogger's performance of progressive social interaction. Through online vlogs, the participants stated that encouragement and support were amongst the most important aspects of the rock-climbing experience. However, some of the participants stated that elitism was a natural part of rock-climbing, due to its competitive edge. This suggested that the competitive and elite nature of rock-climbing accompanies an individual as they expose themselves to difficult rock-climbing routes. 'Intimacy' in a digital and real-life context creates spaces for unique relationships, which leads to exclusive social norms. In this instance, social behaviours arise from competitive norms within spaces of leisure, such as rock-climbing venues.

Social Regulation

Through the theme of social regulation, it became clear that social norms and behaviours also emerge from rock-climbing's individualised and immerse practice. The theme also revealed that the elite nature of various rock-climbing groups is centered around notions of machoism and self-interest. In doing so, the cultural performance of 'showing no fear' has become embedded into the wider context of the modern climbing culture through various climbing artefacts. In this instance, climbing vlogs are seen as a form of cultural resistance through their alternative understanding of rock-climbing's relationship with natural human emotion. However, through elitist social norms, the theme suggested that individuals attach themselves to groups of equivalence inside the cultural experience of rock-climbing. 'Self-interest', and its relationship with Foucault's (2008) neoliberal entrepreneur suggested that some elite climbing groups are still bound to the neoliberal 'frame of mind'.

Conclusion

This study has developed a critical understanding of neoliberalism (Foucault, 2008), risk societies (Beck, 2014), and flow (Csikszentmihalyi, 1990) through the social experience of rock-climbing cultures. The research project used rock-climbing vlogs as a case study to demonstrate that new media is capable of resisting traditional behaviours and social norms. Through neoliberalism, it became clear that modern life prevents individuals from experiencing Csikszentmihalyi's (1990) Flow. This suggested that climbers immerse themselves in flow to resist the risk-averse lifestyles associated with neoliberal values. The study has also revealed that social behaviours also arise from competitive norms within rock-climbing space. In doing so, climbers use social memberships to attach themselves to groups of equivalence. Through this, the study revealed that social interactions impact the wider context of rock-climbing cultures, and finally, that neoliberalism is capable of adjusting an individual's social behaviour.

Bibliography

Agius, S J. (2008) Qualitative Research: It's value and applicability. Cambridge: Cambridge University Press.

Argyle, M. (1994). The psychology of social class. New York: Routledge.

Beattie, P. (2019) The Road to Psychopathology: Neoliberalism and the Human Mind. Journal of Social Issues. 75 (1). pp.89-112.

Beckham Blomquist, K. and Danner, F. (1987) Effects of Physical Conditioning on Information Processing Efficiency. Perceptual and Motor Skills. August. 65 (1). pp.175-186.

Beck, U. (1991) Ecological Enlightenment: Essays on the Politics of the Risk Society. Amherst: Prometheus Books.

Beck, U. (2014) The Brave New World of Work. New Jersey: John Wiley & Sons.

Beck, U. (1994) The Reinvention of Politics: Rethinking Modernity in the Global Social Order. New Jersey: John Wiley & Sons.

Berlant, L (2000) Intimacy: A special issue. In: Berlant L (ed.) Intimacy. London: The University of Chicago Press. pp.1–9.

Berlant, L (2008) The Female Complaint: The Unfinished Business of Sentimentality in American Culture. London: Duke University Press.

Bianchi, R. (2006) Tourism and the globalisation of fear: Analysing the politics of risk and (in)security in global travel. Tourism and Hospitality Research. November. 7 (1). pp.64-74.

Bourdieu, P. (1984). Distinction: A Social Critique of the Judgement of Taste. London: Routledge.

Braedley, S. and Luxton, M. (2010) Neoliberalism and Everyday. Montreal: McGill-Queen's Press.

Branch, J. (2015) Lost Brother in Yosemite. [Online} Available from: <
https://www.nytimes.com/2015/06/14/sports/dean-potter-final-yosemite-jump.html> [Accessed 3rd October 2021].

Bunn, M. (2017) A disposition of risk: Climbing practice, reflexive modernity, and the habitus. Journal of Sociology. 53 (1). pp.3-17.

Cailly, L. (2006). Climbing sites as counter-sites? Essay on neo-community forms and territorialisation processes at work in the practice of rock climbing. Revue de Géographie Alpine. 94. pp.35-44.

Cameron, A. (2020) Coronavirus and homeworking in the UK: April 2020. [Online] Available from: <
https://www.ons.gov.uk/employmentandlabourmarket/peopleinwork/employmentandemployeetypes/bulletins/coronavirusandhomeworkingintheuk/april2020> [Accessed 28th July 2021].

Carpiano, R M. (2009) Come take a walk with me: The "Go-Along" interview as a novel method for studying the implications of place for health and well-being. Health & Place. March. 15 (1). pp.263-272.

Carswell, C. (2015) Death renew calls for national parks to rescind Base Jumping bans. [Online] Available from: <
https://www.hcn.org/issues/47.12/deaths-renew-calls-for-national-parks-to-rescind-base jumping-bans> [Accessed 3rd October 2021].

Castells, M .(1996) The Rise of the Network Society. Blackwell: Oxford.

Chakravarty, U. Chand, G. and Singh, U D. (2021) Millennial travel vlogs: emergence of a new form of virtual tourism in the post-pandemic era? Worldwide Hospitality and Tourism Themes. July. 13 (3). Pp.1-11.

Chesire, L. and Lawrence, G. (2006) Neoliberalism, Individualisation, and Community: Regional Restructuring in Australia. Journal for the Study of Race, Nation, and Culture. August (11) 5. pp.435-445.

Collingwood, R G. (1938) The principles of art. Oxford: Oxford University Press.

Conroy, C. and Gonzalez, G B. (2017) Off Belay! The Morality of Free-soloing. Sport, Ethics, and Philosophy. September. 13 (1). pp.62-77.

Crust, L. (2020) Personality and Mountaineering: A critical review and directions for future research. Personality and Individual Differences. 161. September. pp.1-10.

Csikszentmihalyi, M. (1997) Finding Flow: The psychology of engagement with everyday life. York: Basic Books.

Csikszentmihalyi, M. (1990) Flow. New York: Harper & Row.

Csikszentmihalyi, M. (2014) Flow and the foundation of positive psychology. New York: Springer.

Csíkszentmihályi, M. (1975) Play and Intrinsic Rewards. Journal of Humanistic Psychology. 15. pp.41-63.

Dencker-Larsen, S. Lundberg, K G. (2016) Depicted welfare-recipient stereotypes in Norway and Denmark: a photo-elicitation study. Nordic Journal of Social Research. 7. pp.1-15.

Draper, N. Jones, G A. Fryer, S. Hodgson, C I. and Blackwell, G. (2010) Phsyiological and psychological responses to lead and top rope climbing for intermediate rock climbers. European Journal for Sports Science. November. 10 (1). pp.13-20.

Eldik, A K. Kneer, J. Lutkenhaus, R O. and Jansz, J. (2019) Urban Influencers: An Analysis of Urban Identity in Youtube Content of Local Social Media Influencers in a Super-Diverse City. Frontiers in Psychology. December. 10 (2876). pp.1-17.

Elliot, A. and Urry, J. (2010) Mobile Lives. London: Routledge.

Eriksen, T H. (2012) Means of communication: transnational struggles and scarce resources. Nordic Research on Media and Communication. 33. pp.15-28.

Erickson, B. (1975) Style Matters: Movements of masculine desire in rock-climbing. Ottawa: National Library of Canada.

Featherstone, M. (1985) Leisure, Symbolic Power, and the Life Course. The Sociological Review. May. 33 (1). pp.113-138

Field, D. (2004). Moving from novice to expert: the value of learning in clinical practice:
A literature review. Nurse Education Today. 24. pp.560-565.

Finlay, L. (2021) Thematic Analysis: The 'Good', the 'Bad', the ugly. European Journal for Qualitative Research in Psychotherapy. July. 11. pp.103-116.

Flick, U. Kardoff, E V. Steinke, I. (2004) A Companion to Qualitative Research. Thousand Oaks: Sage.

Foucault M (2008) The birth of biopolitics. New York: Palgrave Macmillan.

Frykman, J. and Lofgren, O. (1996) Forces of Habit: Exploring Everyday Culture. Lund: Lund University Press.

Garrido-Palomino, I. and Espana-Romero, V. (2019) Role of Emotional Intelligence on Rock Climbing Performance. Revista Internacional de Ciencias del Deporte. July. 15 (57). pp.284-294.

Gelfand, M J. (2018) Rule Makers, Rule Breakers: Tight and Loose Cultures and the Secret Signals That Direct Our Lives. London: Little Brown Book Group.

Gleason, T R. Theran S A. and Newberg E M. (2017) Para social interactions and relationships in early adolescence. Frontiers of Psychology. February. 8 (255). pp.1-11.

Goffman, E. (1963) Stigma: Notes on the Management of Spoiled Identity. New York: Touchstone.

Goffman, E. (1990) The Presentation of Self in Everday Life. Harmondsworth: Penguin.

Goudie, R J B. Mukherjee, S N. De Neve, J E. Oswald, A J. Wu, S. (2014) Happiness as a Driver of Risk-Avoiding Behaviour. Economica. 81 (324). pp.674-697.

Grant, B C. Thompson, S M. and Boyes, M. (2013) Risk and Responsibility: In Outdoor Recreation. Journal of Physical Education, Recreation, and Dance. February. 67 (7). pp.34-35.

Griffin, L. (2012) Famous New Zealand climber dies in fall. [Online] Available from: < https://www.thebmc.co.uk/famous-new-zealand-climber-dies-in-fall> [Accessed 21st July 2021].

Guest, G. MacQueen, K M. and Namey, E E. (2011) Applied Thematic Analysis. Thousand Oaks: Sage Publications.

Hanley, T. (2011) Globalisation, UK Poverty, and Communities. [Online] York: Joseph Roundtree Foundation. Available from: < https://www.jrf.org.uk/sites/default/files/jrf/migrated/files/po vertycommunity-globalisation-summary.pdf> [Accessed 8th June 2021].

Hebdige, D. (1979) Subculture: The Meaning of Style. London: Routledge.

Hechter, M. and Opp, K D. (2001) Social Norms. New York: Russell Sage Foundation.

Heider, F. (1958) The Psychology of Interpersonal Relations. New Jersey: Lawrence Erlbaum Associates Publishers.

Heinemann, K. (1980) Sport and the Sociology of the Body. International Review for the Sociology of Sport. September. 15 (3). pp.41-56.

Herrera, C D. (2002) The moral controversy over boxing reform. Journal of the Philosophy of Sport. 29. pp.163-173.

Heywood, I. (2006) Climbing Monsters: Excess and Restraint in Contemporary Rock Climbing. Leisure Studies. 25 (4). pp.455-467.

Hujich, P. (2012) Identifying coping mechanisms: Recognising our harmful coping mechanisms opens the way to greater freedom. [Online] Available from: <https://www.psychologytoday.com/us/blog/mind-wellness-awareness/201209/identifying-coping-mechanisms> [Accessed 27th July 2021].

Hulya Asci, F. (2004) Physical Self Perception of Elite Athletes and Non-Athletes: A Turkish Sample. Perceptual and Motor Skills. December. 99 (3). pp.1047-1052.

Janghorban, R. Roudsari, R L. Taghipour, A. (2014) Skype Interviewing: The new generation of online synchronous interview in qualitative research. International Journal of Qualitative Studies on Health and Well-being. March. 9 (1). p.1-3.

Jenkins, H. Shresthova, S. Gamber-Thompson, L. Kligler-Vilenchick, N. and Zimmerman, A. (2016) Any Media Necessary: The New Youth Activism. New York: New York University Press.

Keinan, R. and Bereby-Meyer, Y. (2012) "Leaving it to chance" - Passive risk taking in everyday life. Judgement and Decision Making. 7 (6). pp.705-715.

Kenyon, G S. (1968) A conceptual model for characterising physical activity. Research Quarterly. 39 (1). pp.96-105.

Kilvington, D. (2013) British Asians, Covert Racism and Exclusion in English Professional Football. Culture Unbound: Journal of Current Cultural Research. 5 (4). pp.588-606.

Langseth, T. and Salvesen, O. (2018) Rock Climbing, Risk, and Recognition. Frontiers in Psychology. September. 9. (1793) pp. 1-10.

LaRose, R. Connolly, R. Lee, H. and Hales, K D. (2014) Connection Overload? A Cross Cultural Study of the Consequences of Social Media Connection. Information Systems Management. January. 31 (1). pp.59-73.

Laval, C. (2017) L'homme économique: Essai sur les racines du néolibéralisme. Paris: Gallimard.

Leeds Beckett University. (2017) Research Ethics Policy. [Online]. Leeds: Leeds Beckett. Available from: < https://www.leedsbeckett.ac.uk/UPethics_framework>. [Accessed 21st February 2022].

Llewellyn, D. and Sanchez, X. (2008) Individual differences and risk taking in rock climbing. Psychology of Sport and Exercise. 9. pp.413-426.

Llopis-Goig, R. (2016) Sports participation and cultural trends. Running as a reflection of individualisation and post-materialism processes in Spanish society. European Journal for Sport and Society. March. 11 (2). pp.151-169.

Luckin, R. and Weatherby, K. (2014) Online learning communities in context. International Journal of Web Based Communities. October. 8 (4). pp.440-454.

Luttenberger, K. Stelzer, E M. Forst, S. Schopper, M. Kornhuber, J. and Book, S. (2015) Indoor rock climbing (bouldering) as a new treatment for depression: study design of a waitlist-controlled randomised group pilot study for the first results. BMC Psychiatry. 15 (201). pp.1-10.

MacLeod, D. (2020) How to climb trad #3 Resilience. [Online Video] September 2020. Available from: <https://www.youtube.com/watch?v=B6gAC2YWXLU> [Accessed 29th December 2021].

Marcus, B. Weigelt, O. Hergert, J. Gurt, J. Gelleri, P. (2016) The use of snowball sampling for multi-source organisational research: Some cause for concern. Personnel Psychology. May. 70. pp.635-673.

Mascarenhas, M. (2012) Where the Waters Divide: Neoliberalism, White Privilege, and Environmental Racism in Canada. Minneapolis: Lexington Books.

McDonald, M. Gough, B. Wearing, S. and Deville, A. (2017) Social Psychology, Consumer Culture and Neoliberal Political Economy. Journal for the Theory of Social Behaviour. February. 47. pp.363-379.

McLuhan, M. (1964) Understanding Media: The Extensions of Man. New York: McGraw-Hill.

Moscovici, S. (2001). Social representations: Explorations in social psychology. New York: NYU Press.

O'Dwyer, M. Singh Warich, M. and Jain, H. (2016) India as I Knew it. Sahibzada Ajit Singh Nagar: Unistar Books.

Oogjes, D. Fung, P. Odom, W. (2016) Designing for another home: Expanding and Speculating on Different Forms of Domestic Life. Expanding Domestic Design. June. 9 (13). pp.313-326.

Orth, D. Davids, K. Chow, J Y. Brymer, E. Seifert, L. (2018) Behavioural Repertoire Influences the Rate and Nature of Learning in Climbing: Implications for Individualised Learning Design in Preparation for Extreme Sports Participation. Frontiers in Psychology. June. 9 (949). pp.1-20.

Peachey, K. (2021) How Covid has changed where we want to live. [Online] Available from: < https://www.bbc.co.uk/news/business-56359865> [Accessed 16th November 2021].

Pinson, G. and Journel, C M. (2016) The Neoliberal City - Theory, Evidence, Debates. Terroitory, Politics, Governance. February. 4 (2). pp.137-153.

Pizam, A. Neumann, Y. and Reichel, A. (1979) Tourist satisfaction: uses and misuses. Annals of Tourism Research. 6 (2). pp.195-197.

Raunch, S. Wallner, B. Strohle, M. Das Cappello, T. and Brodmann-Maeder, M. (2019) Climbing Accidents: Prospective Data Analysis from the International Alpine Trauma Registry and Systematic Review of the Literature. Int J Environ Res Public Journal. January. 17 (1). p.203.

Read, J. (2009) A genealogy of homo-economicus: neoliberalism and the production of subjectivity. Foucault Studies. February. 6. pp.25-36.

Robinson, D W. (1985) Stress Seeking: Selected Behavoural Characteristics of Elite Rock-Climbers. Journal of Sport and Exercise Psychology. 7 (4). Pp.400-404.

Robinson, V. (2008) Everyday Masculinities and Extreme Sport. In Wheaton, B. (2007) After Sporting Culture: Rethinking Sport and Post-Subcultural Theory. Journal of Sport and Social Issues. 31 (3) pp.283-307.

Rokeach, M. (1973) The Nature of Human Values. New York: Free Press.

Russell, J S. (2005) The value of dangerous sport. Journal of the Philosophy of Sport. 32. pp.1-19.

Salmons, J. (2014) Qualitative Online Interviews: Strategies, Design, and Skills. Thousand Oaks: Sage.

Sanchez, X. Boschker, J S. Llewellyn, D J. (2010) Pre-performance psychological states and performance in elite climbing competitions. Scandanavian Journal of Medicine and Science in Sports. March. 20. pp.356-363.

Scott, D. (2021) That feeling when... What? Sport society, and emotions. In: Reid, B. and McKee, T. eds. Dualism: Confronting Sport through its Doubles. Champaign: Common Ground Research Networks. pp.1-18.

Sherry, J L. (2004) Flow and Media Enjoyment. Communication Theory. November. 14 (4). pp.328-347.

Silverman, D. (2020) Qualitative Research. Thousand Oaks: Sage.

Simon, J. (2001) Embracing Risk. Chicago: University of Chicago Press.

Sparkes, A C. and Smith, B. (2016) Routledge Handbook of Qualitative Research in Sport and Exercise. London: Routledge.

Toh, S M. and Leonardelli, G J. (2012) Cultural Constraints on the emergence of women as leaders. Journal of World Business. 47. pp.604-611.

Tyler, I. (2020) Stigma: The machinery of inequality. London: Zed Books.

Uhrig, M K. Trautmann, N. Baumgartner, U. Treede, R D. Henrich, F. Hiller, W. Marschall, S. (2016) Emotion Elicitation: A Comparison of Pictures and Films. Frontiers in Psychology. February. 7. (180) pp.1-12

UKC (2003) Elitism [Online] Available from: < https://www.ukclimbing.com/forums/rock_talk/elitism-65574> [Accessed 24th December 2021].

Wenger, E. (1998) Communities of Practice. Cambridge: Cambridge University Press.

Wenger, E. (2011) Communities of Practice: A Brief Introduction. Step Leadership Workshop. October. p.1-7.

Wenger, E. and Snyder, W M. (2000) Communities of practice: the organizational frontier. Harvard Business Revie. 78 (1) pp.139-144.

West, A. and Allin, L. (2010) Chancing your arm: the meaning of risk in rock climbing. Sport in Society. September. 13 (7). pp.1234-1248.

Winlow, S. and Hall, S. (2006) Violent Night: Urban Leisure and Contemporary Culture. Oxford: Berg.

Xu, D. Chen, T. Pearce, J. Mohammadi, Z. and Pearce, P L. (2021) Reaching audiences through travel vlogs: The perspective of involvement. Tourism Management. April. 86. pp.1-12.

Zillman, D. (1994) Mechanisms of emotional involvement with drama. Poetics. (23) pp.33-51.

Zuckerman, M. (1994). Behavioural expressions and biosocial bases of sensation seeking. Cambridge: Cambridge University Press.

Appendix 1: glossary

What is a climbing route?

A climbing route (also known as a 'line') is a vertical path which a climber uses to reach the top of steep terrain.

Climbing grade

Climbing grades determine the difficulty of a specific climbing route.

Climbing venue

A climbing venue refers to space dedicated to the practice of rock-climbing, this can be found in an indoor and outdoor context.

Exposure

On the 'path' of a climbing route, specific sections involve exposed parts where there is an increased risk of injury if the climber were to fall.

Protection

Protection refers to the technology which climbers use to place protection gear, which catches the fall of the climber.

Bolting

The modern approach for some climbing routes involves drilling a fixed bolt into the rock as a permanent form of protection.

What is a climbing project?

Projecting involves dedicating days, weeks, months, or years into a climbing route that is above an individual's physical limit.

Flash

A Flash is when a climber completes a route in one attempt.

Belaying

Belaying is a rope technique used to control the fall of a climber.

Spotting

'Spotting' is carried out during the practice of outdoor bouldering; ropes are not used. When the climber falls, the spotter directs the climbers fall onto protected padding.

What is beta?

'Beta' is the term used to describe the techniques and methods used to ascend a climbing route.

What is an on-sight?

'On-sighting' is when a climber leads a route on their first attempt without any prior information or advice about the route. This is similar to the 'flash' attempt, but is a term used in longer routes which involve rope, rather than bouldering.

First ascent

A first ascent refers to the first successfully documented ascent of a climbing route.

Appendix 2: participants

None of the photographs used in this section are photos of the participants who took place in this study. These images have been used to replicate the lifestyle and experience of the anonymous climbers who chose to participate in this study.

1. Max is a 35-year-old male from Yorkshire. He regularly engages with risk-induced free-soloing at local venues after work.

2. Asha is a 24-year-old male from Carlisle. He spends his weekends in the Lake District free-soloing routes that he has previously ascended with protection. Whilst doing so, Asha participates in bouldering competitions at his local climbing wall and spends his spare time off the wall watching vlogs, films, and documentaries about climbing.

3. Zoe is a 19-year-old female from Oslo, Norway. She trains at a local wall with her girlfriend for their yearly deep water soloing trip in Spain. Deep water soloing is similar to free-soloing, however, the

climber lands in the water below the climbing route if they were to fall.

4. Eleanor is a 31-year-old female from Yorkshire. Most of her climbing goals revolve around pushing her indoor climbing grades whilst maintaining her non-climbing career goals.

5. Alex is a 26-year-old female from Northumberland. She spends most of her time climbing outside on low-ball boulder problems. A low-ball boulder problem refers to a climbing route that is low to the ground without too much risk if the climber were to fall. Although Alex prefers to climb by herself, she also participates in women's socials events at her local climbing wall.

6. Alistair is a 38-year-old male from Valencia, Spain. He spends his year training at indoor and outdoor venues, so he can climb at his physical limit. Alistair has a small social circle of experienced climbers. Alongside this, he prefers to engage with other climbers through vlog comments and forums.

7. Marian is a 52-year-old woman from Yorkshire. She spends most of her time climbing outside with her partner. She has built a climbing wall in her garage so she can commit to outdoor climbing without investing in a membership at an indoor climbing wall.

A note about Boom Graduates

Around the world – including wherever you are now - there is a huge social mobility problem. Students are missing out on education because there are not enough funded scholarships for disadvantaged students, including the poor, the neurodiverse, the disabled and oppressed. Moreover, institutions are missing out on unique researchers that have the ability to blow the academic roof off their research departments.

We are Boom Graduates - an imprint of Boom Publications Ltd. We are a more-than-profit company, dedicating over half our profits to providing university scholarships for underprivileged students across the world. We aim to become the globe's biggest provider of such scholarships – and if like Matt, the author of this book, you'd also like to contribute to social mobility, please contact us: we publish monographs, edited books, and moreover our graduate series – Boom Graduates – are presented at graduation days across the world in archival, lined museum-quality presentation cases, engraved with the graduate's name and award.

We are also climate conscious and work with agencies to plant a tree for each and every book commissioned, offsetting thousands of tonnes of carbon each year. Follow us on social media to watch our forest grow @boomgraduates.

Thank you for contributing by purchasing this book. Please visit our catalogues on www.boompublications.com.

BOOM!

This book was originally submitted as a dissertation in partial fulfilment of the requirements of a Masters of Arts degree in Media and Culture at Leeds Beckett University, UK.

108

109

www.ingramcontent.com/pod-product-compliance
Lightning Source LLC
Chambersburg PA
CBHW070135260726
48658CB00001B/428